For Elzbi
Best wi
Deborah x

Curiosity –
An Effective Way
to Empower Patients

– DEBORAH TRENCHARD –

An environmentally friendly book printed and bound in England by
www.printondemand-worldwide.com

Mixed Sources
Product group from well-managed
forests, and other controlled sources
www.fsc.org Cert no. TT-COC-002641
© 1996 Forest Stewardship Council
FSC

PEFC Certified
This product is
from sustainably
managed forests
and controlled
sources
PEFC
PEFC/16-33-415
www.pefc.org

This book is made entirely of chain-of-custody materials

www.fast-print.net/store.php

Curiosity – An Effective Way
to Empower Patients
Copyright © Deborah Trenchard 2013

A catalogue record for this book is available from the British Library

ISBN 978-178035-605-1

First published 2013 by
FASTPRINT PUBLISHING
Peterborough, England.

Disclaimer

The author is not medically trained and does not give medical advice or prescribe the use of any method in this book as a replacement for medical treatment. She recommends that patients discuss their concerns with their doctors or hospital consultants/physicians. The author is dedicated to the promotion of curiosity as an effective way to help patients harness their inner power.

In memory

Dr Hugh John Trenchard FRCP (1913–1988), to whom I am exceedingly grateful for showing me the way.

Tiffany Sophia Trenchard (1985-2006) whose short life made such a positive impact on mine

My Deepest Gratitude

To those without whom this work would not have been possible: the women and men who were willing to be interviewed; the members of the public I'd talk to on the streets or in hospital waiting rooms who shared their views on being curious patients; questioning doctors, and the NHS. And the friends who called me at the first sighting of an article or TV programme they felt would be of interest to me.

I'll always be indebted to my neighbour and friend Dr Alan McClelland, Consultant Paediatric Psychiatrist whose support – as he lay on his deathbed – allayed my fears when I discovered I had to have cardiac surgery. "Go for it," he would encourage. "Heart surgery today is a doddle. You have nothing to fear. In six months' time you'll have a new life; in six months' time I'll be dead." I did; and he was.

Special thanks to my editors, and hard task masters, Andy Taitt in Barbados and George Hill in London, for pulling me up when I was slacking, or being sloppy! I'd also like to thank Lesley Butler for taking some time from her busy schedule to offer her proofreading skills. _Lesley@puppetplanet.co.uk_

Praise

Deborah Trenchard has a wealth of experience as a carer, patient, and hospital volunteer. She also has the skills to impart her knowledge to others in an effective and supportive way. She is a motivating and inspiring individual.

Elizabeth J Haxby, MBBS, MA, MSc, FRCA
Lead Clinician in Clinical Risk
Royal Brompton Hospital, London

No one is more aware than Deborah Trenchard of the problems carers encounter looking after children with disabilities. I have known her for more than twenty years, and observed her energy, determination and resilience at firsthand. She is a marvellous communicator and to be in her company is stimulating and uplifting.

Michael L Rigby MD FRCP FRCPCH
Consultant Paediatric Cardiologist,
Royal Brompton Hospital, London

Deborah is a vivacious, extrovert and enthusiastic woman. One who makes others feel good about themselves. Knowing her as I have over the past twenty-five years, she's always brimming with positive energy. With her vast experience as a patient and a carer her commitment to empowering others within the healthcare system is unremitting and profound. Deborah is a great inspiration to others.

Dr Jane Mounty, Consultant Psychiatrist, London

Deborah Trenchard is a phenomenal woman: kind, insightful, tenaciously optimistic. Her charm and positive energy make working with her a boost for the spirit, as well as a productive process for the mind. Deborah's wealth of experience makes her a life coach you can rely on whatever your life circumstances.
Dr Martha Beck, Sociologist, Life Coach and NY Times bestselling author

Deborah is enthusiastic, positive and lively. She also has a genuine interest in people. Her spontaneous way of getting patients together and helping them to feel optimistic during her hospital visits was inspiring to everyone.
Eve Cartwright, PALS Manager, NHS, London

Comments

"**Y**our booklet is a most eloquent and moving account of your own experiences and I am sure is very valuable to other patients as well...The insights offered would, I believe, be of wide benefit."
Katherine Murphy, Chief Executive,
The Patients Association

"**I** have been an in-patient in two London teaching hospitals, at one for three months and at the other for just under two. I cannot stress sufficiently the importance to the patient of being pro-active. It is more important to fully understand one's own treatment and condition than to try to placate those treating us with an ingratiating smile. Not all consultants' technical skills are matched by their communication skills. It is up to us, as patients, to keep them on their toes. Deborah reminds us how this can be done."
Rosalind Hadfield, North London

"**T**his is a wonderful, thoughtful piece about the patient's part in healing him or herself. I profoundly agree with you about the extra ingredient of gratitude. We lack it in our society and I noticed only recently how I lack it in myself. Now I've noticed, I can see how much there is to be grateful for every day. I'll share this with my surgeon brother – who would be surprised if any patient asked him how he was. But he'd be awfully grateful!"
Fiona Anderson,
retired television writing coach, London

"Your book gave me so many moments of joy. I was touched by the way you skilfully communicated your depth of experience and knowledge in a light-hearted compassionate tone. You tread the path of being inclusive, not taking sides, 'exceedingly' well. On behalf of all those who are patients at one time or another, I am very grateful that you made the effort to share your experience, knowledge and wisdom."

Patricia MacDonald, counselor, London

"I'm blown away by this. Not only by your life experiences, caring for Tiffany and your own surgery, but by the sensitive and intelligent way you create the soup! Life is indeed a learning, and gratitude for the simple things essential – from oxygen to human kindness!"

Rowena Coxwell, potter, France

"I agree it is important that you are more proactive with your health. I'm healthy, but I'd like to think that I would be a curious patient. It is human nature not to realise what you've got until it's gone. Many people do not appreciate the NHS."

Lorna Kwenda, South London

"I remember when Neil and I bumped into you at the Royal Brompton Hospital a couple of days after eleven-week-old Olivia's heart operation. It was all so raw. You said to me 'Question, question, question…' I haven't stopped questioning since, at every appointment. She is incapable of taking control as a patient. As a mother, I represent Olivia's best interests, and with the greatest trust for, and support of, the medical team we have met so far. You've also reminded me to get a grip and take control of my own health issues, too."

Suzanne Furmston, Hertfordshire

Contents

Introduction

Over the years patients have shared their feelings of loneliness with me. This seems to be the case even if they are sitting in the vast outpatients' area waiting to be called. For a great many, it seems, illness can be a dark, confusing, and fearful place, creating in its wake a life-state of powerlessness and lack of hope. But I've also noticed that once someone reaches out and encourages them they relax and open up; a new mindset emerges.

Seven out of ten people I've asked have said they never question their doctors' authority. Instead, they leave the consultation room somewhat confused. Interestingly, they've said that they usually have a burning question for their doctor or surgeon, but once face-to-face they feel intimidated, fear takes over and their insecurities kick in. And this is one of the main reasons for writing this book; a source of encouragement told from a patient's perspective. I share ways patients can ignite their curiosity and, not only understand their illness a bit more, but discover its source.

Remember the saying "Curiosity killed the cat"? The theory behind this centuries-old proverb is unclear. One source says it was a physicist who was behind some experiment. Whatever the case, I am encouraging you to go down a dark alley; even if you are afraid of the dark! You'll be amazed at what you'll find! And besides, about that cat; legend has it that "satisfaction brought it back". Incidentally, the word satisfaction – from its Latin origin – means: *satis* 'enough' and *facio* 'to make, do, create'. Can you recall a moment when you'd achieved something in spite of the obstacles you encountered?

Here is something else for you to explore: "Everything is energy." Ancient mystics knew this. Now, today, modern philosophers along with a growing number of scientists are making us more aware of this concept. A common example of this energy is electricity. We cannot see it, but when we flick the switch, it appears. We sometimes also talk about feeling people's vibes (negative or positive). This is another form of 'energetic vibrations', or 'non-verbal' communication. Did you know that only 20% of our communication is spoken? The other 80% is expressed through our physical behaviour or body language.

Try to recall a time when someone voiced or reacted to something you were thinking. You probably wondered how that person knew. Or a time you walked into a place and instantly felt that something 'wasn't right' or something 'spoke' to you in a positive or happy way. Today, in the world of complimentary and holistic medicine you will find various techniques and methods of energy healing, energy therapy and energy medicine.

So what about the severely disabled person or the person who has had a serious accident and is lying unconscious in the intensive care unit, or a baby? Having had a disabled child and experienced those in similar or worse physical, and or, mental conditions, I learned that their hearing and understanding is much greater than we think.

There are numerous ways we can, and do, communicate. We are unable to get in other people's heads and see what they are thinking. This doesn't mean that they are not hearing and understanding what we say or feeling the energy we are putting out. I've seen severely disabled children, some with no physical movements, others hardly able to blink an eye or even fully blind, yet they showed signs of laughter or sorrow and understanding. In some cases, people communicate through touch, energy. Those working with severely disabled people can attest to this.

Finally, "Seek and ye shall find." This well-known biblical saying teaches us that unless we 'seek' (search for) we will not 'find' (discover and learn) the life and health we would like. Another aspect of the word 'seek' is curiosity: to be diligent. Curiosity is a natural emotion of investigation and exploration. It's having an open mind, taking a risk; going beyond one's self-imposed limitations and misguided beliefs. We see this behaviour in babies and small children.

A four-year-old wouldn't hesitate to ask: "What is that? "What are you doing?" Without any prompting a child would say: "I don't understand." Usually, the parent responds by saying: "Don't bother the doctor (or whoever it happens to be) He/she's a busy person." Some might even say:

"You ask too many questions." Some parents even tell their children to "shut up or else".

Walking through the park the other day I overheard an argument between a mother and her son, who was about three. She was slowly walking in one direction, but he was determined to go in the opposite. "Come on," the mother called. "I want to find another way home," he yelled. "No. We are going this way. We always go home this way," she responded. "No. I want to find another way home," he protested. Reluctantly, the little chap turned his tricycle round and followed his mother. His desire for a new discovery was squashed.

Continuing on my walk I wondered, and not for the first time, if incidences like these are the beginning of the death of our inquisitiveness? The little boy wanted to 'find' a new route home. He wanted to 'seek'; step into the unknown. His mother clearly didn't. This is the beginning of the end of that which lies at the heart of human development. Inquisitiveness is our human right.

Whether you read this book from cover-to-cover, select a chapter or two, or dip in and out, I hope you will be inspired by some of the personal insights and experiences and become explorers of life once again. It is never too late to champion your own human rights.

The Idea

"The fool wonders; the wise man asks"
- Benjamin Disraeli (1804-1881)

During my years as a hospital volunteer, I took a keen interest in patients' involvement, or lack of it, in their own health. In my element, I would encourage them to take a deeper interest in their health. My enthusiasm became more of an obsession. As a result, I was approached by one of the consultants and asked to write a chapter, *The Expert Patient,* for a medical publication she was editing.

Disappointingly, the first draft of the chapter I'd written was rejected. As it was for medical students, a version with historical facts, technical information, and so on demonstrating the doctor/patient relationship and the benefits of patient involvement, was required. I had to rewrite it.

To do nothing with the original document would have been equal to taking all the meat off the bone (no offence to vegetarians!) – the ingredient that adds enormous flavour to the soup – and then throwing it in the bin. What a waste! Incidentally, my former brother-in-law, a retired doctor, to whom I'd sent both versions, said he preferred the original.

With that endorsement I set about creating this patient-friendly version, highlighting some of the common fears patients have, as well as some of the benefits to be gained by being informed and by building better relations with healthcare professionals. From personal experience, this 'learning' can be extremely beneficial.

Soup, as we all know, is the 'putting together' of different ingredients: a splash of this, a dash of that, to make the dish 'just as we'd like it'. And that's precisely what I've done, or tried to do, with this book. I've used various resources (ingredients), starting with my own experience, and added other people's. I've taken from conversations with doctors and other healthcare professionals. I've also been inspired by ideas from books and articles as well as other resources on the subject of patient education and patient empowerment. As I gauged the mood of patients one thing became quite clear: the need to move beyond doubt and fear and expand their mindset. In order for this to be effective they will need to be Equipped, Engaged, Empowered and Enabled. In other words, we need to be Educated. I'm not referring here to academic education; this is not about being book smart. It's about discovery, learning, being prepared, and having the courage to participate. Awareness is a very powerful tool.

Before I go any further, I'd like you to take a moment to ponder the word which will crop up from time to time: FEAR. Fear can be described as feelings of distress or alarm at 'dangers' we think are about to happen. A great many people have a fear of the dark, for example. Yet, when light illuminates the dark they realise that there was nothing there to fear; the monster wasn't real after all! It was 'all in the mind'. There is always something, or someone, we will fear. Fear is intimidating; and over time, we cultivate the habit and become so worried and anxious it is crippling. Though sometimes, and in some instances, the reasons to fear can be justified. If a snake or alligator suddenly appears in your path fear will make you run like hell!

More specifically, I am referring to our fear of the medical establishment, our fear of doctors; and the fear of knowing the facts about the state of one's health. Because of our learned behaviours, we dread the things we do not know; we fear the things we cannot see. Be daring. Take courageous action and unleash your curiosity, step-by-step. Practise courage. It's good for your health!

Are you ready to experience something new, something different? Then, please join me as I prepare the soup – a recipe for the curious process!

Getting Involved

"Fear not my friend, the darkness is gentler than you think."
- Ben Okri, Nigerian author

My aim in writing this book is to help patients understand why it is necessary to make an effort – even when this isn't natural to them. As I mentioned earlier, we don't have to be book-smart or medically literate to cultivate a sense of curiosity when it comes to health. Nor should we feel embarrassed or ashamed because we don't know or don't understand. It's not a classroom situation.

Dr Bernie Siegel, a retired American surgeon, once referred to patients who are curious, who feel empowered, the patients who take their health seriously and go beyond their fear of doctors, as *exceptional* patients. Such patients make an effort to communicate effectively with their medics and ask appropriate questions. With a degree of confidence, they seize every opportunity to learn something more about their condition, and what on-going action they should take. In other words, they are keen participants in their healthcare. And from my ongoing research, this attitude is what doctors would like to see more of. Some have told me it would make their jobs easier.

I'm not medically trained. Nevertheless, I've been fortunate to have had a number of doctors and other medical professionals in my life. Some were neighbours, some spouses of close friends, some in-laws. A proportion of what's written here is based on our conversations over the years. It would have been a waste if I hadn't added their comments and concerns – their own special ingredients – to the soup!

In addition to the three years I worked as a volunteer at the hospital where my daughter Tiffany had been a patient, and where her life came to an end, I spent a large part of twenty years sitting in hospital waiting rooms. During those years I had endless opportunities to engage with consultants, other healthcare professionals, as well as patients. This invaluable experience gave me an even greater insight into patients' fears, real or imagined. Broadly speaking, we fear the unknown or that which we imagine. And even the slightest ailment can cause some people great anxiety. We picture ourselves devastated by a stroke or that the perceived illness will leave us less than 'normal'. We fear the possibility of having some form of cancer because of our family history. We panic, become anxious.

And, for example, if your consultant or physician says that your condition has deteriorated and surgery must be considered, or that the lump in your breast has spread, or your newborn has a life-threatening illness, it is only natural not to hear the rest of his words because in that moment you blink rather than think. You stop breathing; your heart skips a beat; your senses shut down, momentarily. The question you were thinking of asking has disappeared. However, once over the shock it is advisable to know the facts; it is crucial to understanding the problem. And if you don't understand the explanation or diagnosis given, ask and ask again – even if what you hear is frightening. It is always better to know. As Marie Curie once said "*Nothing in life is to be feared. It is only to be understood.*" But in order to understand we first have to know.

When my daughter Tiffany was in the intensive care unit at St Thomas's Hospital the consultant catalogued his suspicions. Just the word 'suspicions' sent shock waves through my body. I thought I'd given birth to a freak. Thus, in that moment, I'd rather not have known. Yelling 'NO MORE PLEASE!' was what I wanted to do. Be that as it may, I had to listen.

"I'm sorry to have to give you such unwelcome news", the consultant said, again.

"Thanks. It's better to know." My words were barely audible.

And this is what most of us are afraid of: knowing. Knowing the facts takes us from a place of denial or complacency and smacks us blatantly across the face with the harsh truth. It wakes us up, propels us to a place of hopelessness and despair, a place of deep pain and penetrating grief, and for some, a place of shame and mortification. Not the best place to be, emotionally.

At one point I wondered how difficult it must have been for the consultant, too. When I went to see him some years later and after Tiffany's death, he told me that doctors have been verbally and/or physically assaulted for sharing their unpleasant findings with parents.

The importance of getting involved in one's health, as part of a collective effort, cannot be emphasised enough. Quietly hoping the pain and discomfort one is feeling would somehow go away having been told something might be 'wrong' is nothing short of being in denial. Sometimes time is not on one's side.

Patient Education

"Education is the great engine of personal development."
- Nelson Mandela, Notes to the Future

Patient education is the way forward. If we are to 'shed light' on our problems, build our confidence, participate intelligently in our healthcare, be positive examples to our children and their children; if we are to build a healthier society, a healthier Britain, then **we must** treat patient education as a priority. Let me remind you again, I am not referring to classroom learning. I'm referring to an open mind. This must come before shopping, mindlessly watching television, or lounging around in negative, toxic behaviour complaining that the government or those around you aren't making you happy, or solving your problems. No longer can you sit back bathed in ignorance; no longer can you sit in front of your doctor and just nod or say "I don't know". Or tell yourself "he knows what he's doing so I let him get on with it."

Knowing about the problem is fundamental to the solution; it is crucial to your healing. And it begins with you – the patient. Perhaps if patients educated themselves and participated more there would be shorter hospital waiting lists, less GP visits; less blame placed on the government; less criticism of the health service. Do you ever feel grateful for our health service? Do you realise how fortunate you are to have such easy access to it? Do you ever stop to think that you, the patient, have the capacity to play a vital role in the improvement of it? You are not just a patient, a dependent on the system; you are a partner in the firm called the National Health Service.

President John F Kennedy, in his 1961 inaugural address, famously urged his fellow Americans to *"Ask not what your country can do for you, ask what you can do for your country."* It is now time that British people were encouraged to think and act along the same lines regarding the NHS.

In January 2011 I wrote to Health Secretary Andrew Lansley, copied to David Cameron and Nick Clegg, suggesting the idea of *PATIENT EDUCATION* as a process that will engender curiosity, which will invariably lead to patient empowerment and in the long-term would be more effective than spending cuts. As a matter of fact, it would save to government hundreds of millions over the years. There is never only one way in any situation. All possibilities must be explored, the letter said, and the process must be on-going and frequently reviewed. I sent a similar letter to the Jeremy Hunt, the current Health Secretary in his request for 'public input'. Needless to say, I didn't get a response from any of the above, personally, but the Department of Health did respond. Instead of it being a deterrent, I became even more committed to this project. The truth of the matter is governments can't do everything; we each have a unique part to play. Perhaps we should ask ourselves: Are we doing all we can to help build a better healthcare system?

We often hear the word 'crisis' when it comes to the 'shake-up' of the NHS. Surely, patient accountability for their own health should be a part of the shake-up as more and more patients contribute to the waste in the NHS by taking the 'easy' or, as one woman put it, 'envied' access to health care for granted. Some examples of misuse would be:

- Allowing drugs to go beyond expiry dates
- Missing costly hospital outpatient and/or GP appointments
- Not taking responsibility for diet
- Lack of exercise
- Smoking
- Excessive drinking
- General lack of interest in one's own health – "the doctor will sort me out" attitude.

Time and time again successive governments have failed to address patient responsibility. Maybe now is the time for our coalition government to break with tradition and explore new ideas; be forward thinking, exploring the idea of promoting greater patient involvement.

A retired doctor once told me, *"I would say that curiosity is an option and choice rather than an obligation."* Surely one has an obligation to oneself to understand, if only slightly, something about the medical condition from which one is suffering.

One effective remedy, I believe, is communication: listening, speaking; all parties engaging in dialogue. Another is clarity. Patients should pinpoint the problem and write it down beforehand, if necessary. Preparation is powerful. You'd be surprised how much we can discuss and learn in ten minutes if we are clear, if we are prepared. This technique will help the patient to get straight to the heart of the matter, instead of nervously waffling on; or just nodding and agreeing with the doctor. I appreciate the fact that this isn't possible for everyone to do. Some people are limited by their age, disability, or language skills. In such cases a relative or patient advocate – someone to speak up and speak out on the person's behalf – is essential.

What if that person lacks the confidence to communicate? Then I'd suggest they read this book!

Doctor/Patient Relationship

*"The doctor-patient relationship is a sensitive one,
requiring respect and openness on both sides."*
Dr Nancy Snyderman, M.D. –
Medical Myths that can Kill You

As if on a mission, I took it upon myself to find out why people feared healthcare professionals, and why they like to be 'told' rather than to 'participate'. In my initial survey I questioned approximately 150 women and 25 men across the spectra of age, background and profession. I questioned patients in hospital waiting rooms, on the wards, on the street and via email. I posed the question to people from the US, Sweden, Barbados, South Africa and Switzerland. I spoke to patient organisations and had a word with a couple of friendly pharmacists.

The pharmacist – the one person seen by patients as 'approachable', I've discovered – finds that patients are eager to chat and discuss their requirements and voice their concerns with him, and do so with great ease. Some pharmacists said they believe the 'fear' lies within the class divide, the educational differences, and the 'intimidation' these pose.

"Let's face it," one person said, "most doctors, English especially, are from middle-class backgrounds. It is obvious then that this snootiness plays a huge part when it comes to their work. It is who they are. Some of them treat patients is if they were just case histories."

I discovered that even some middle-class patients are equally intimidated in these situations. One day after listening to patients, some of whom were highly educated professionals, on my 'ward round' as a volunteer; it occurred to me that perhaps most people are afraid of sounding stupid. "Go on, sound stupid!" I would urge.

I decided to cast my net wider and seek out someone whose job it was to help 'shape' Britain's National Health Service. I emailed Edwina Currie, former Health Secretary in Mrs Thatcher's government. She listed the doctor/patient relationship problems as:

- Deference – doctor knows best.
- Fear – if I question the doctor he/she may take umbrage and not be kind.
- Superstition – if the doctor lets slip too much, the knowledge may be bad for me.

"It is not a relationship of equals," Mrs Currie went on to say. "A great number of patients are (i) elderly, and so brought up to be deferential to authority; (ii) less well educated; and (iii) too ill and/or worried."

She continued: "Many doctors are hurried, rude, awkward, and not interested in answering questions. For dialogue a patient needs knowledge, time, curiosity and self-confidence; doctors need common understandable language, compassion and judgement."

A great many patients have told me how arrogant and ill-mannered their GPs and hospital consultants are. "They never look you in the eye; they never apologise, either," some shared. They certainly never say: "I made a mistake." Why?

The pharmacist is not the only professional patients feel relaxed with. Phlebotomists (those trained to draw blood from a person) also have a tale or two to tell. One once told me that she has always been baffled as to why patients leave the doctors' office to then ask her to explain what's written on the request form. They would ask why their doctor has requested this or that blood test. What does a 'fasting blood test' mean? "I'm not a doctor," she would respond. "Why didn't you ask the doctor while you were there?" She said she noticed the fear and incompetence of a many patients. "At least the older ones have an excuse. In my thirty years in this job nothing has changed. It's getting worse. I know it's because they are afraid of the doctor. And to be quite honest with you, some doctors are intimidating; they think they're gods, which doesn't make it easy for their patients, either." So why does a doctor write a prescription or a blood request form without explaining to his/her patient?

"A good doctor is one who listens to and embraces patients with compassion. He/she should ask gentle, probing questions; even try to put him/herself in the

patient's shoes." These were the words of my late father-in-law during one of our doctor/patient discussions.

A compassionate doctor should also extend an invitation to his/her patients by asking: "Is there anything you would like to ask me?"

Medical Jargon

According to a medical journalist I spoke to, "There is a need for the doctor/patient partnership to be one of equals... Doctors will have to cease using medical jargon. It intimidates patients."

Being told there is something seriously wrong, with very little explanation and in a language people cannot understand – or conversely, being given too much information – is overwhelming. A patient must be ready, emotionally, to hear and take in the information given by the doctor. This means it may be necessary to impart relevant facts and details about prognosis and treatment in several stages. Whatever information the doctor is about to impart, it can be frightening. And because patients expect to hear the worst, it renders them vulnerable, susceptible to memory loss, quaking knees and deep worry.

Even when patients are encouraged to "question their doctors" (in accordance with NHS leaflets), they still find it difficult. Too many patients just nod and take their doctor's word for everything. They leave the consulting room fretting, lost or confused, fearful. This is commonly referred to in America as 'the white coat syndrome'.

This is especially true when healthcare staff use jargon and acronyms, language that is foreign to patients. A doctor's telling his patient, with very little explanation, that he has to have a 'TOE[1], or that the Echo[2] shows

---

[1] TOE: Transesophageal echocardiogram is a medical investigation using an ultrasound probe passed through the oesophagus, or gullet, to take images of the heart (source Wikipedia).
[2] Echo (echocardiogram) an ultra-sound based technique used to create images of the heart (source Wikipedia)

there's an 'AF[3]', can cause a rise in the patient's blood pressure and prompt feelings of fear and insecurity.

A woman told me about the letter she received from her gynaecologist about the analysis of polyps removed from her cervix. This middle-age woman has a history of cancer and both her mother and sister had died from the disease so she was naturally terrified. The consultant informed her of an abnormality called *complex hyperplasia without atypia*. At her follow-up appointment the woman spoke with the female doctor about the usage of jargon.

"Not everyone has a medical dictionary or access to the internet,' she told her. 'This kind of information scares women."

To which the doctor responded, "We use medical terminology in order to have a discussion with patients when we sit with them in clinic." Perplexed, the lady told the medic that, "It's not a discussion if you alone have the knowledge."

One can imagine a patient's anxiety in between appointments having received such a letter. This is an exquisite example of the doctor/patient barrier. This midlife woman felt the consultant's letter should have said: "The result of the sample shows a condition known as *complex hyperplasia without atypia*. This simply means you have patches of thickening cells of the womb due to a lack of progesterone. It is complex because you have a lot of it. Usually, none of the cells are malignant or of the sort that are likely to turn malignant."

Undoubtedly, a doctor's response must be crystal clear, and so must the patient's questions. We assume. Doctors, too, assume. They assume that if patients do not respond intelligently, or at least attempt to do so, to what they are telling us then we understand, or would rather not know. This is when we must challenge our perceptions, our assumptions. Assumptions leave us in the dark. Whereas questioning someone – in this case your doctor – honours that person, their professionalism. Suddenly, they become more available to listen, to engage, to prompt. The doctor sees the patient as someone who is making an effort and responds in kind. This is the point where a discussion develops. The doctor/patient relationship is born and both feel less burdened.

---

[3] AF: Atrial fibrillation is an abnormal heart rhythm - a quivering of the upper heart chambers (source Wikipedia).

A Break with Tradition

Having established that the doctor/patient relationship is inextricably linked, there will have to be changes on both sides. For this to happen there will have to be a break with tradition: the thing we've always known; the behaviour we've always displayed, etc. When patients sit in front of the consultant, the last thing on their minds is the physician's state of well-being, whether they may be running out of steam, whether they'd had a dreadful row with their spouse, or children, before coming to work. Perhaps they were going through a divorce. Or drowning in the paperwork of NHS bureaucracy. These are all things that need to be considered. Ask your doctor how he or she is today.

Dr Bernie Siegel, a retired American paediatric surgeon, in his book *Love, Medicine and Miracles*, encourages patients to greet their doctors with a hug. I'm not sure how well that idea would go down with English doctors! After my former GP's wife died I would ask him how he was. A couple of years later he told me that I was the only patient who expressed an interest in his well-being. I once asked an audience of around one hundred people – some teenagers – if they ever asked their doctors how they were. One brave lady stood up and said she didn't know she could. "Try it," I said. "This approach immediately creates a different kind of doctor/patient relationship."

When I took Tiffany, aged eighteen at the time, to see her new consultant at the Royal Brompton Hospital, he introduced himself as Michael. This casual greeting immediately puts a patient at ease, it breaks down traditional barriers, it invites a patient to ask a question, and without fear.

This must be the way forward, because I've noticed that some junior doctors introduce themselves by their first names as well.

Not all consultants are distant or unapproachable. Bar one unpleasant experience with a consultant many years ago, I have tremendous respect, not only for those who cared for my daughter for over twenty years, but for my personal physicians, too. After Tiffany's death I returned to the hospital to thank her consultants, some of whom I had known all her life. And each tête-à-tête was a unique opportunity to sit and laugh and share, openly. We shared feelings, projects, personal opinions and experiences. Most of the conversations had nothing to do with their professional lives. They expressed an interest in my life after Tiffany. I've since asked those consultants for personal endorsements. They were delighted to do so.

One forty-something patient shared with me her unique experience with consultants at two different hospitals. "They are most approachable," she said. "We're like old friends. We talk about families and holidays, even our stress levels, before getting down to the business at hand!"

It is clear therefore, that change has to come from both sides. Patients can no longer sit feebly when they consult with their physicians. They will have to learn to master the art of speaking up and speaking out. Crucially, doctors will have to be less intimidating and more embracing by developing their communication skills. And from what I've learned, this is changing. More and more medical schools are no longer selecting tomorrow's doctors based solely on their qualifications. Applicants are now tested on their people skills, their communications skills.

Good social skills are crucial if doctors are to be more approachable; if they are to break with tradition. Too many have a reputation for being insufferable know-it-alls who bully nurses and mostly ignore their patients. This new procedure will have tremendous benefits; not only for the new medics and patients, but for the entire healthcare system.

Asking the Right Questions

One morning, as I stood at the window mindlessly looking at the sky, out of nowhere popped the memory of one of the smartest young women I met during my years as a hospital volunteer. Mary, I'll call her, suffered from cystic fibrosis. Cystic fibrosis is a genetic disorder – an illness caused by abnormalities in genes or chromosomes – mainly affecting the lungs, also the pancreas, liver and intestine. Patients with this disease are usually on a cocktail of drugs, as well as oxygen. Mary, twenty-three, was supremely confident and humourous in spite of her illness and the fact that spent more time in hospital than out. One morning the pharmacist arrived at her bedside to inform her of the changes her consultant had made to her drugs. Like a lawyer, she demanded answers to her burning questions:

- Why hasn't my consultant (calling him by name) informed me and discussed it with me first?
- Will this new medication interfere with what I'm currently taking?
- How long before it kicks in?
- And what are the side-effects?
- How long will I have to take it?

Why am I telling you this story? Mary, who sadly lost her life to her disease two weeks later, was an exquisite example of curiosity. She was an 'expert' patient. Why expert? Patients like Mary are engaged with their healthcare professionals, they question, they discuss. Consequently they learn everything about their illness. We can all learn from them. Four years on, I still use Mary's experience to encourage people. People who believe they aren't in charge of their life; people who feel so miserable that unlike Mary, they can't see anything to laugh about. She gave me something truly valuable. It was one of the great benefits of volunteering. Little did I realise then how much sitting and chatting with patients would positively impact on my life.

Mary's attitude was a stark contrast to Joyce, the patient I met when I was in hospital in October 2010. I'd gone in for a series of tests after my annual echocardiogram showed there was a problem with my aortic valve, replaced twelve years earlier. One of the tests was carried out under general anaesthetic. Later that afternoon one of the consultants came to see Joyce, the patient diagonally across from me, a woman in her early forties. After some time watching her reaction to some 'not very good' news, I approached her bed. She motioned for me to sit.

"You heard," she began.

"Yes I did. How are you feeling after that?"

And with that Joyce began to cry. I held her hand and told her that crying was healthy. "No need to apologise for being human," I said, jokingly.

She explained that she'd had a procedure the previous year that had corrected one thing, but had damaged another, leaving her with very little movement on her right side. She'd been on a number of drugs to try to correct the problem. The consultant left her with a couple of options. She discussed her options with me and said the thing she feared most was leaving her ten-year-old son behind.

I shared with her my story which I wrote in my first book, *Finding Me – a Life in Transition*:

Just before my cardiac problem was diagnosed I couldn't explain my tiredness. On my way to a meeting one Sunday morning I got out of the lift and flopped to the floor. Alone and scared in this ancient building, my teeth chattered like false teeth in a pantomime. I thought it was the end. My life flashed before me. Leaning my limp body against the wall I could only think about my children, Tiffany especially. I was suddenly tormented by the question: who would care for her? Seemingly from nowhere I gathered strength, raised my body, and walked ever so slowly down corridor into the room....

After hearing my story, Joyce asked what she should do. I don't give medical advice. Therefore, the question wasn't mine to answer. "Why didn't you come right out and ask the consultant that all-important question, 'If you were in this situation, Dr Johnson (not his real name), what would you do?'

"I couldn't possibly do that," she said, "although it was at the tip of my tongue. You don't ask doctors those questions."

YOU DO!

The afternoon (in 1998) I met my surgeon to discuss my impending valve replacement surgery, he said I didn't have to choose the type of valves I'd like to have there and then. "You have until the day before the operation to make your mind up," he said. When that day finally arrived, having researched my options – I wanted to avoid taking Warfarin (also known as Coumadin) – we discussed biological valves. "Because of your age, chances are, I'll have to operate again in five years' time."

I wasn't keen on that idea. "If you were in my situation, which would you choose?"

Without hesitation he replied "mechanical valves." And that was that. "So Warfarin it is then." We smiled.

Using my life coaching techniques I took Joyce through a series of questions. Every time she evaded the issue I would rephrase the question. What we were discussing was her attitude – based on our social beliefs – and NOT her medical complications. At one point she realised the connection between the negative things she had been hanging on to since childhood and her health, which was why she couldn't question her consultant in 'that way'.

To her, Dr Johnson was 'an authority figure' like her father. I asked her if she was aware that her father was still ruling her life, her every move, every decision she made? Through a veil of tears, Joyce admitted that this had always been the case. It is a very important question to put to any doctor, "If it were you what would you do?" Or, "Would you recommend this treatment for your wife, your child or elderly parent?"

Indisputably, the majority of us were brought up not to question 'authority figures'. Some say it's rude, while others believe it isn't polite. From a certain age the words we hear most often are *don't, can't, shouldn't*. Having this societal belief drummed into us throughout our lives we lose the sense of curiosity we had as babies, as young children.

No one asks more questions than an inquisitive four-year-old. He will ask why, or how come, until he's satisfied with the answer. Parents usually respond by saying, "Why do you ask so many questions?" Or, "Why do you need to know?" It's as if questioning is bad for us.

Think for a moment how it would be if parents encouraged their children to ask the doctor a question or two, instead of planting seeds of fear. A sixty-plus woman told me that her mother had "instilled fear of doctors in her". Thankfully, I am healthy, so there is no need for me to *ever* visit a doctor," she said emphatically. Coincidentally, this woman's husband has heart problems. When she speaks about it one senses nothing but fear and anxiety.

Are You in Denial?

Let's look for a moment at the dictionary's definition of the word denial: *psychological process by which painful truths are not admitted into an individual's consciousness.* In other words, one tries one's hardest not to hear, see, feel or speak the truth in the hope that by 'not facing the situation' it will somehow vanish into thin air. This act of denial is sometimes referred to as 'brushing it under the carpet'.

Tiffany was born seven weeks premature. She weighed just over four pounds. We were told by the health visitor – a woman whose conviction gave us hope – that our daughter's slow growth was due to her prematurity. That's what I believed; that's what I hung on to. We all like to be reassured. Without question, there had been 'signs'. Tiffany's development wasn't like her older brother's.

I didn't know what those signs meant, nevertheless they were there: Tiffany's large head, her disproportionate limbs, dysmorphic (or abnormal) features, her inability to suckle properly, and more. When the consultant rattled off these deformities, his 'suspicions', somewhere deep within I would rather have hung on to my belief that they were 'because she was premature' than 'signs of disability' and other 'medical complications'.

And that's what denial does: it says I'd rather not... This act of 'looking away', not wanting to confront the aches and pains, the rash, even, can sometimes have irreversible consequences. Too late. All because we are afraid to look, ask, confront the disease, and face the truth. We then blame the doctors for our ignorance.

Once I'd come to terms with my reality I rose to the challenge. It wasn't a matter of 'why me', but 'try me'. I vowed to use what I endured, what I learned, to encourage others. Most of what I've shared is based on the knowledge I've gained having faced the truth, having freed myself from the clutches of denial, the clutches of fear.

The consultant's findings were correct – my daughter was disabled, there were medical complications such as a missing kidney, a form of dwarfism, congenital heart disease and pulmonary hypertension (high blood pressure in the lungs). This complex heart and lung malfunction, known as the Eisenmenger syndrome, caused her blood to flow around the body in the wrong direction. As a result, her blood was insufficiently oxygenated thereby limiting her physical activity. Her feet, fingers and lips would go 'blue', a condition called cyanosis. Babies born with it are referred to as 'blue babies'.

It's better to know. "But it's scary," the young woman I was coaching said. "What is the alternative?" I asked. "Will not knowing make it better or go away?" Yes, it is scary. The heart races, the fingers shake, we're even lost for words, but it is wise to avoid avoidance! It is not a healthy option. Simply trying to shun any issue one might find challenging is the same as being in denial, which is based on fear of the unknown.

Let's look at a simple and effective (step-by-step) process to help you move from denial to acceptance, at least a better understanding:

• **FEAR** — how many times have we heard people say they "worried for nothing"? You expect to hear or see the worse, the most frightening, which in turn creates stress, which then creates ill health. There is a Buddhist saying: *"If the problem can be solved, there is no use worrying about it. If the problem can't be solved, worrying will do no good."*

• **TRUST** — this means having the courage to 'let go'. Trust says 'stop worrying' and take the necessary steps to go beyond one's limiting beliefs. There is an answer to every situation. Some people are comforted by the thought "something good will come out of this."

• **CUROSITY** — learning something about your condition or situation. Curiosity means that you have an enquiring mind. A curious person understands the value in knowing.

• **PARTICIPATION** — when you are curious you have the courage to participate in your health issues. This gradual process begins to build confidence.

• **CONFIDENCE** — you are no longer blaming and complaining. Instead, you are taking positive action and moving in a 'healthy' direction. At this point you have the courage to ask your doctor: "Is there anything else I need to know?"

• **EMPOWERMENT** — strength, optimism, compassion. And because you are taking responsibility, you are no longer afraid to discuss your test results, or question your physician or surgeon; the 'white coat syndrome' is no longer an issue. An empowered person expresses gratitude and joy; she sees the cup as half-full, **not** half-empty.

How would you describe your cup?

Feeling Intimidated

One morning in December 1985 I rang for an ambulance. Tiffany, seven months old at the time, had gone blue, her body limp. It was a terrifying experience. She was immediately admitted to St Thomas' Hospital in London where she spent three days in the intensive care unit.

During my first meeting with her consultant he explained, in minute detail, what was wrong with the tiny girl whose disproportionately large head was in a transparent box inhaling 100% oxygen; any less and she would go blue. Anything I couldn't comprehend he would draw on a piece of paper. As I said in an earlier chapter, there were so many things wrong it was overwhelming. This was when my twenty-year journey as an out-patient parent began.

My father-in-law, a retired hospital consultant at the time, accompanied me for the first two years of that journey. He would sit and observe the consultants and then share his thoughts: whether they were being compassionate or arrogant. "Question, question, question," he would instruct. "Never leave a consulting room with a burning question on your mind. Questioning is another way of learning."

One day Tiffany's consultant at St Thomas's, aware of my still feeling insecure because of my lack of knowledge, said to me, "I'm an expert when it comes to medicine; you're an expert when it comes to your daughter." From that moment on he and I worked as a team.

Since then, I would naturally encourage patients to cultivate this attitude as we sat in hospital waiting rooms or on the wards in my capacity as a volunteer. I'm always shocked by the disproportionate number of patients who do not question healthcare professionals, especially their doctors and surgeons. Some even accept the change of medication without asking why, or what the side-effects are.

And when it comes to 'meeting with the surgeon', the very person patients should be questioning, having a dialogue with, they quake at the knees. They nod and don't, as a rule, ask the all-important questions. Perhaps they emotionally disconnect out of fear of the unknown, or what's about to be revealed might be too complex and complicated for them to comprehend. This is a natural reaction.

The surgeon, the so-called 'powerhouse' of the operating theatre, the man/woman wearing the 'Badge of Honour', as it was once referred to, is undoubtedly the most feared. Some believe it may be the air of arrogance some exude. It is possible that for many patients a surgeon seems unapproachable simply because he is referred to as Mr (in the UK) rather than Dr. Added to this, the unfamiliar environment of a consulting room often has patients feeling intimidated, overwhelmed, consumed by fear. Whatever the reason, most patients still arrive for their appointment ill-prepared to ask relevant questions regarding the surgery they are about to undergo, or the illness that's about to be investigated.

Some people will say that they've already 'checked it out' on the internet. A woman told me this having spent a number of years taking her ten-year-old son to the hospital for his congenital heart problem. Time and time again, feeling dissatisfied with the answers given by his consultant, coupled with her fear of questioning doctors, she would go home and 'try to understand' by surfing the internet.

Not everyone is internet savvy. Not everyone knows what to do with the information that pops up on their computer screen. One important thing – doctors have told me – is the relationship patients need to build with their consultants as they sit one-to-one. Dialogue is essential. Even if, like the mother above, we know, in theory, what the problem is. Although she got most of the answers on her computer screen, something was still missing. She was sad. Feelings of emptiness and "letting her son down" engulfed her. She admitted being scared to ask, to admit she didn't understand, for fear of looking stupid. Unknowingly, she'd been carrying her childhood fear of teachers and those in 'authority'. Psychologically, she was still in the classroom. Thus, she was still afraid to 'put her hand up' and ask another question for fear of being 'told off' or ignored.

Our Fear of Doctors

"The cave you fear to enter holds the treasure you seek."
- Joseph Campbell (1904 – 1987) an American Mythologist

Now let me share a personal experience of fear. In 1981 I met and married a middle-class Englishman. I mentioned earlier that his father was a retired hospital consultant. This novel and exciting experience placed me in a situation I had never dreamt of and that seemed surreal from my poor Caribbean background. My brother-in-law was also a doctor. Suddenly, I was on familiar terms with two 'authoritative' men. The kind of superior figures my social class said I should fear and yet respect. Confusing, to say the least, but that's what they taught us.

According to social beliefs doctors are professionals you visit when you are ill in order to get well. They're certainly not people you sit at the same dinner table with. In my colonial upbringing, English doctors were to be revered; and even more so if your mother or aunt happened to be his house-servant and your uncle or cousin his gardener. Pedestal, pedestal, pedestal – that's where doctors belonged. Although generally not easily intimidated by authority, the day I was to meet my future father-in-law I awoke a nervous wreck. When introduced to this 'mighty man' I quaked inside; I would address him as Mr Trenchard as opposed to Dr Trenchard.

Some years later when I asked a professional woman in her mid-forties what she thought about the doctor/patient relationship, whether patients should take a greater interest in their health, she said, "I think doctors are a symbol of trust and knowledge. To question them erodes the patient's sense of security, as well as their expectation that 'doctor will fix it'".

She went on to say, "My father was a general practitioner. He would be horrified, if he were alive today, by the lack of communication between physician and patient. My experience has been horrendous. They [doctors] do not read your notes before you arrive, which can lead to poor diagnosis and embarrassment. They don't seem to be able to listen at all, which is an important factor in diagnosis. When a patient questions them, they skip over it as if your understanding of your own body is rubbish."

A sixty-something retired woman shared a similar dissatisfaction with her doctor. "I no longer question my hospital consultant," she told me. "Previously, when I asked, he would give me the impression that it wasn't terribly important for me to know. I have now taken my health into my own hands. I go online and check out my symptoms on the internet."

We expect doctors to know everything and we're deeply horrified and disappointed when we find out they don't. In the mid-Eighties I took my severely handicapped daughter back to Great Ormond Street Hospital for the results of some chromosome tests. Sadly, there was no name for her condition, consequently no cure. And the biggest shock came when the consultant told me they were only able to correctly diagnose 40-45% of the cases that came through the door.

My dear friend Jane is a consultant psychiatrist. When I asked her if she feels intimidated when she visits her GP, she said her main concern whilst there is that her allocated minutes are running out. I posed the same question to a female consultant cardiologist. She told me that as a doctor she encourages her patients to question her. "I extend an invitation for them to question me, to find out more about their condition. But when I am on the other side of the stethoscope, I am a nervous wreck. I want to leave without taking up too much time. Consequently, I leave having not had a discussion about what I was there for in the first instance."

By the way, another meaning of the word 'doctor' is teacher. Another definition of doctor comes from the Latin verb *docēre*, meaning 'to teach'. So in essence, our doctors are our teachers of medicine. They should, therefore, clearly explain the procedures and conditions that we, the patients, do not understand. It is equally important that patients play their part, too. One idea as suggested by Dr Mehmet Oz, an American heart surgeon, is for patients to write down the questions and concerns they would like to discuss with their physician and give the doctor a copy. He believes this 'checklist' to be an effective way for patients to overcome their fears and connect with their doctor.

Below is Frances's story of her fear of doctors and why she made the decision to be proactive:

"Thank you for your article on patients' fear. It has helped me to recognise the source of my own fear of doctors and medical intervention and the authority that doctors appeared to have over me.

"When I was eight years old my mother took me to the family doctor who towered over me as he examined my throat and pronounced that my tonsils and adenoids would have to come out. I can still recall the dread that those words produced. I felt as though my blood drained from my body and, totally helpless, I felt like I was being sucked into a vortex of black nothingness — unable to think and powerless to control what was happening to me.

"In due course I was taken, like a lamb to slaughter, to the local children's hospital and prepared for the operation. Even now, I remember clearly the bright red blanket on my bed and the sickly-sweet smell of ether as my nose and mouth were covered with a black rubber mask. I awoke to find myself in the ward with matron sitting beside my bed — her starched white apron and my snowy bed-sheets covered in blood. Apparently, I had bled profusely and needed a transfusion. My throat was packed with gauze and it was difficult and painful to swallow.

"It was the first time I had ever been away from my home and family and, under such fearful circumstances, the emotional pain of separation from my mother was more intense than my physical discomfort. The whole experience laid down in my psyche a morbid dread of medical treatment. Strangers invading my body with instruments, without my permission, as if it was their domain and I had no control over what they decided to do with it.

"I grew up in an era when it was unthinkable to question the decision made by the doctor, or the treatment prescribed. At school, we were vaccinated en masse without a choice to opt out. When I had my two children, because I had a less common blood type, I was told I 'had to' have a serum injection and regular fortnightly blood samples taken during my second pregnancy. Again, there was no question of discussion about it. It was just taken for granted that the medical professionals knew best and one did not question their authority.

"Now, at age 67, I have learned to trust my own instincts and to take responsibility for my own health. Recently, while registering at the local doctors' surgery, I questioned the practice nurse as to whether the blood samples she was about to take (as a formality) were really necessary. She said no, it was just standard procedure. I said that, in that case, I would prefer not to give samples. I felt happy that I was taking responsibility and making my own choices and decisions about what I allowed to be done to my body.

"So, thank you Deborah for helping me to move from fear to understanding and the knowledge that, if I need to seek advice from a doctor in the future, it will be my decision whether or not I follow it."

Where Does Our Fear Come From?

"Do the thing you are afraid to do,
and the death of fear is certain."
- Ralph Waldo Emerson, 19th century
American philosopher and poet

Let's take a closer look at some of the common fears people have: heights, water, snakes, spiders, flying, mice, aging, dying; and most people are terrified to speak in public. In today's society there is the fear of terrorist attacks. There is also people's fear of the dark, social rejection, and the unknown. To this list I would add doctors, surgeons, and dentists, injections, awaiting a diagnosis, being alone, losing money – or not having enough of it. Debt, too, terrifies people. On the other hand, some fear can be good. For example, you would take the necessary precautions to protect a small child from harm. If you are terrified of things going wrong in your life fear can prompt you into taking positive action. But in this chapter I'll be talking about the fear that holds people back, keeps them from experiencing the unknown and living life to the full.

According to *Wikipedia*, the online encyclopedia, *"fear is a distressing negative sensation induced by a perceived threat... Fear is apparently a universal emotion; all persons, consciously or unconsciously, have fear of some sort...Whatever its source, it can become a controlling factor in a person's life."*

Like malignant cancer cells, fear can have devastating consequences; not only on our health, but it spreads to other areas of our lives. Fear, whether or not we are aware of it, influences the way we live our lives – from the decisions we make to the friendships we have. It also determines the attitude with which we go about our daily lives. I've learned through psychology and spirituality that it is an illness – an illness of the mind – not to be confused with mental illness.

Fear is created primarily by one's negative thinking; how we perceive something or a situation to be, as opposed to what is real. Unaware of this, we then behave according to those negative instructions: what if this or that happens? What if the tests reveal a lump, or diabetes, or a rare genetic disorder? What if I have to have heart surgery? What if my husband has another heart attack? Some people would rather stay in ignorance.

We fear losing the job, the house, the spouse and money. People worry about what will happen if something bad happens. We fear being out of control, being mugged or burgled. Some are even afraid of meeting new people, while others are suspicious of their neighbours and/or strangers. We live in a society that breeds fear, resentment and suspicion. Trust is seriously lacking these days. Such is the case that we are unaware of the depth of its effects. As a result people blame, especially the government, for not doing enough, not giving enough; they dump personal responsibility on others.

These are some examples of the thoughts and beliefs that trigger panic, anxiety, stress and raise blood pressure, or cause some to overeat, or eat the wrong food, as a way of 'calming' themselves down; a way of 'dealing with the problem'. On the contrary, it's the highway to high cholesterol levels, Type 2 diabetes, heart problems, depression, and low self-esteem, to name a few.

Like all behaviours, whether negative or positive, fear has a root. Some people believe that having lots of money will make them happy. It won't. Money buys material things, which inevitably leads them to quibble over ownership: this is mine that is yours. Most of the truly happy people I've ever met were poor. They welcomed people into their homes with open arms, love, story-telling, and laughter; the elders were honoured; they lived in harmony with nature. Others talk about money being "the root of all evil". What if the root of all evil is fear?

Because we are afraid to do so many things (this behaviour is very subtle and often presents itself as an excuse) we stop ourselves from achieving our full potential. For instance, when we were little we were extremely inquisitive and totally unaware of danger. So we touched the flaming stove or the flickering candle and got burnt; we fell down stairs and got hurt. Quite naturally, our parents rushed to protect us from harm. And of course this should be the response of any responsible adult. This is called normal fear. Unconsciously, their nervousness and fear extended to other areas of life too: doctors and hospitals, losing money, especially if you were poor; the hoarding of possessions, and on and on the list goes. In other words, they dealt with the situation by using the conditioning that was handed down to them.

Some people believe that more than fear of doctors, dentists and death is the fear of losing money; the fear of being poor, or not having enough. And this attitude applies to the wealthy as well. They are afraid to trust anyone with their money, especially if they'd had a negative experience. Somewhere in their psyche they doubt money will ever come their way again. Borrowing money from a relation or a close friend can cause an untold amount of shame, anger and resentment for some.

Have you noticed the number of houses on our streets that are fitted with burglar alarms and CCTV cameras? Just about every high street has security cameras. Within the past ten years we've seen the rise in requests for CRBs (criminal record bureau) when applying for jobs, voluntary work; working with the elderly, children and the disabled. And in some cases this is necessary. But now, even to babysit, terrified parents want to know that you are not a paedophile. Britain is said to be the most monitored country in the world; all in the name of 'security', 'protection'.

Embedded in the new British passport is a chip that, in a sense, tags the holder. The politicians would have us believe that 'tracking' people is "in the interest of national security". Let's not forget that the people who represent us in Parliament bring their learned fears, and behaviours based on what had been instilled in them, too, to the Cabinet Office. The same applies to those who treat us medically. Teachers haven't escaped this negative input, either. Basically, we were all taught more or less the same basic fears; the same basic morals – the dos and don'ts about life; the same basic values, and equally, the same suspicions. The big question is: do members of the public feel less fearful being surrounded by all this 'security'?

Taking the fear discussion a bit further, what about the person who is afraid to put herself forward for a promotion, or apply for a job that calls for one qualification more than she has, in spite of the fact that she has years of experience? The same could be said of those who write the book, only to put the manuscript in the bottom drawer for fear of rejection by publishers. They fear it won't be good enough. This behaviour is primarily from past memory – the root. "You are not bright enough", or "You don't have what it takes", even though you may have years of experience. And this is a biggie: "Why can't you be like everyone else?" They are those who say, "I've learned to keep my mouth shut". We're also afraid of criticism, it hurts too much.

Because of this ingrained fear of disappointment, of 'getting it wrong', we're afraid to take a risk, step out of the box or try something different, something new. As children we had injections (vaccinations), or a bandage had to be removed from a wound; even when the doctor placed his stethoscope on your chest mum tried to comfort by saying: "Don't worry; it's not going to hurt." Perhaps you recall hearing these words: "I fear the worst." Doctors tend to say, and in a very formal tone, "It's not good I'm afraid", or they tell you to "expect the worse". Two words pollute our lives consistently are, "I'm afraid". It is a very British thing to say. "I'm sick with worry", is another expression of fear, anxiety.

Finding the Courage

"You have to be the expert on your own body."
- Dr Mehmet Oz, Professor of Surgery at Columbia University, New York

Being told there is something wrong with your heart is frightening; to learn that your heart muscle has been damaged, even if only slightly, and you don't know anything about it, is alarming. This is what happened to me in 1995. Not only was I experiencing unusual tiredness, in the evenings, especially, there was a rattle on my chest that caused me to cough nonstop. One morning in the wee hours my heart slowed down to a dangerous level. Frightened, I sat up. The coughing continued and I decided to go to the bathroom to check what I was coughing up. I was horrified at the sight of bright red blood. Too frightened to wake my husband I remained sitting until day break. After showing him the piece of tissue I'd spat in, equally horrified, he immediately rang his brother. By this time the coughing had stopped. My brother-in-law suggested a number of things it could have been, namely pleurisy (a chest infection) and urged me to get to my doctor.

A couple of days later my doctor – who had previously diagnosed my symptoms as the flu – sent me, as a matter of urgency, to the hospital after the X-Ray revealed a serious problem with my heart. You can imagine the fear that overpowered me as I sat in the hospital waiting to be called. The echocardiogram revealed heart valve corrosion, caused by childhood rheumatic fever. This was shocking news to me. I recalled having an illness of sorts when I was around eight or nine that my grandmother had diagnosed as pneumonia. Consequently, I had no reason to tick the box on the medical form that indicated rheumatic fever. Self-diagnosis was a common practise when I was growing up in the Caribbean during the fifties. This experience has taught me that self-diagnosis (guesswork) is DANGEROUS. Although the elders did get it right most of the time. Still, it is wise to know for sure what you are treating.

Although the prescribed diuretic did its job in draining the fluid from my lungs, two years later tests revealed that the condition of my valves had worsen. Looking at my ECG (echocardiogram) results that morning the cardiologist broke the news: "Your valves are now badly damaged, and if you don't have surgery soon we won't be able to help you." I'd heard similar words ten years earlier from my daughter's cardiologist: "I'm terribly sorry Mrs Trenchard, but it is not possible to correct Tiffany's problem." Naturally, as a mother, those words overwhelmed me with fear and disappointment. Nonetheless, someone else's medical prediction, no matter how close the relationship, isn't the same as one's own.

Back to my own diagnosis. Walking back to my car that sunny morning I wanted to scream. I sat in the car for a few moments, my body shaking with fear, trying to comprehend what had just been said to me. It seemed surreal. I was under the illusion that I was tired and slow, but there was nothing to be concerned about. Obviously, I was in denial. Etched somewhere is my psyche was my childhood belief that just some of this or that would make it go away. And the fact that the doctor had mis-diagnosed the problem didn't help, either.

Once home, instead of screaming I called my neighbour, a doctor, who was being challenged by his own medical nightmare – pancreatic cancer. "You have nothing to fear," he consoled. And would, little-by-little, explain heart surgery to me, though he was not a cardiologist. This one-to-one learning experience helped me to develop my confidence; I was no longer jittery about going under the knife. Not everyone will have such an opportunity, but people have the ability to do their own research and consult (seek advice from) their doctors and surgeons; or perhaps those who have had a similar experience.

Concerned about the waiting list, he would urge me not to worry: "You're in the system somewhere. If it was urgent we would not be having this conversation." We shared life stories, hopes and dreams, music; we would discuss politics; we would even try to 'put the world to right'. We laughed a lot, even when just about everything became an effort for him. Our families grew closer.

One morning, feeling hellish and in deep pain, he rang and asked if I could drive him to the hospital. He wanted to talk. During the journey he shared some of his fears. We both got very emotional as he reached out and held my hand. "I hope the cancer hasn't returned," he said, tearfully. Sadly, it had. And upon my return from his funeral some weeks later, there was a message on the answering machine from the Royal Brompton Hospital offering me a date for my surgery.

It wasn't only the doctor who had encouraged me during that time. My ex-husband taught me how to research some of my questions on the internet. I also read lots of spiritual and self-help literature; I read other people's positive experiences and set about applying some of the techniques they used, like meditation, to my daily routine. Every morning as soon as my family had gone, I would sit and stare out of the window at the beautiful gardens, the trees, the sky; my eyes and thoughts would follow all activity; moving from this position was difficult sometimes. Friends, too, played a huge part by offering their support. By the time I was due to have surgery in August 1998, I was ready! Then my initial surgery time was cancelled minutes before I was due to be taken to the operating theatre.

Although disappointed, I didn't fret or blame the surgeon or criticise the health service. The surgeon had had an emergency during the night. An emergency by its very nature means there is a crisis at hand. In the end, I felt pleased that I was well enough to allow someone else, who was obviously dangerously ill, to go first. I believed that if we were both in danger one of us would have died; this way we both lived. So, instead of complaining and engaging in any negative talk about the health service, and waiting lists, etc, I simply used the three weeks to the next date to enrich my life. Spend quality time with my family. Initially, my ex-husband was riddle with anxiety. It had brought back memories of his diseased father and his heart condition. But hours after my cancellation he looked at me and said: "I'm proud of the way you handled the situation; your optimism is infectious."

On that sun-drenched September morning I walked out of the Royal Brompton Hospital a new and unstoppable woman; a woman on Warfarin; a woman proud of her scar! My recovery was swift. A couple of weeks after I ran for the bus! It was only after I hopped on that I realised what I had done. My new sense of power and vitality drove me to start executing some of the ideas I had been dreaming of. Cardiac surgery changed me to the point where the impossible felt like nothing. And it was this experience, more than any other that I would share with patients during my stint as a volunteer. They said how much my enthusiasm had lifted their spirits.

After my surgery I returned to the hospital and thanked my surgeon, his registrar, my cardiologist and the nurses. I did the same after my daughter died. Gratitude is an essential component to healing.

You, too, have the ability and inner skills, to go beyond negativity and doubt. It is the start of the healing process – the new belief that there was nothing to fear after all. And because of this we cheat ourselves of a full life. In her book *Feel the Fear and Do It, Anyway*, author Susan Jeffers urges her readers to do just that – do it, anyway.

Hope and Health

During my research I found that men were the ones least willing to share their stories. Harold, a man in his mid-sixties, was an exception. He told me how petrified he was of developing Type 2 diabetes. *"I have to drag my heavy feelings of fear and despair to a place of hope. I am determined to keep this inherited infliction at bay. There is nothing more terrifying than waiting for my blood test results,"* he said. *"But I'm becoming a smarter patient by being more and more aware, by educating myself. I'm making diet and exercise a priority. It isn't easy, but I'd rather 'give up' certain foods, than 'give in' to medication."* Then he added, *"Medication is more of a bandage because it dresses the wound. It doesn't actually deal with the real cause."*

Martha, an American woman I contacted as part of my research, sent me the following in an email: *"You wanna know how I deal with my fears surrounding cancer and ultimately death? I think it's more to do with our fear of death that eats us up. What's the point of lamenting and going on and on about 'Why me?' It is me. So once I accepted the diagnosis I started to search for positive likeminded people. I insisted on the positive mindset because there is nothing more depressing than hanging out with a bunch of negative 'poor me' folks.*

"I found a group. I didn't know there were so many sick folks within a ten mile radius of my house! This made me realise how people want to hide away once they're ill, as if they feel it's something to be ashamed of. They are about 12 of us between the ages of 40 and 83 with all sorts of problems. A problem shared is a problem halved. It's wasn't easy to bare one's soul to a group of strangers, but I had to get over it! We laugh a lot; drink endless cups of herbal tea and coffee; sometimes we indulge in a glass or two of wine and some delicious food! Why should we give up everything? A bit of this and that doesn't hurt. Just don't overdo it!"

Martha went on to say, *"It's tough when you're told you have cancer, or diabetes; when your doctor scares the hell out of you with the news that you have something incurable, or a condition you hadn't a clue about, how lonely a space that creates. And if your spouse, or close friend, dies suddenly, you think that it'll be you next. Dwelling on it, living in fear, only make things worse. So we read books, listen to medical and nutritional experts, we even listen to some motivational speakers. It wakes us up.*

"Of course I was angry at the beginning. I couldn't cope. I had to ask myself: who are you blaming? With whom are you angry? And this is why some sort of positive support system is essential.

"As often as I can I go and sit in nature; it's the best cure for me. Though sitting and listening to the birds, etc, hasn't cured my cancer (yet!) it has cured my fears, my resentment, and my frustration. My head clears and I have some very profound insights. I find reasons to laugh, reasons to live. It's still hard sometimes. I also write down whatever I am thinking as I sit quietly looking at the trees. Anything is better than another drug. It's a healthier option. It lightens the load, and hey presto, the fear disappears! And that's the joy of having the emotional and moral support of a group. Family tends to worry about you, but in the group everyone's positive and hopeful.

"Human beings tend to hide when something is wrong because of pride and shame, and all that negative stuff, but being open and sharing is far better than moaning and complaining and getting all depressed. We look forward to our monthly get-together. We express our gratitude for life; we live in hope; and even commit to ticking off at least one thing from our 'bucket list' – no matter how small. Best of all, no one judges you."

Martha is a superb example of someone who, with an open mind and positive support, not only released herself from the prison called fear, but has continued to live with hope and optimism.

Why not join a patients' group? Ask your doctor's surgery if there is one in your area. If there isn't, suggest the idea. Also, there are groups that 'walk for health'. If you are not aware of one, ask around, form one. Start with a couple of people. Years ago I moved back to Barbados. On my walk early one evening I approached the young woman who was power walking on the other side of the road and asked if I could join her. She led the way through little villages and roads I would not have known otherwise. Little children would cheer us on! Not only was I now commitment to walk 3-4 times a week, but I learned about my new neighbourhood in the process.

Remember, this book is about curiosity; about breaking new ground and moving from the familiar – the comfort zone – to something new and challenging. This is your opportunity to kick up an inner emotional storm – so 'just do it'!

Be a Smart Patient

1. Prepare for your appointment by learning something about your condition before visiting your doctor, hospital consultant, or any health clinic.
2. Arrive at your appointment at least 20 minutes early. Instead of fretting, or being anxious, bring a book or magazine to read (preferably something light-hearted) while waiting. This should help calm your nerves.
3. Write down at least one question you would like to ask. Tell yourself, I want to know. Being in denial, trying to shun the truth, is unhealthy.
4. Once called, say "Good morning/afternoon" to your doctor. "How are you today doctor?" This gesture is unimaginably powerful. It helps release fear and begins to build confidence.
5. When your doctor asks how you've been, or how you're doing, don't start with a complaint. Instead, tell the doctor what you've observed about your illness.
6. If the doctor or nurse uses medical language, say, "I don't understand. Please explain it to me." If you cannot grasp the explanation, say so.
7. Ask if there is anything else you could do (other than, or in addition to, medication) to improve your condition.
8. Always check the details on the blood request form, or prescription. Mistakes are often made.
9. Think of someone you know, or perhaps have seen on television, that has had a positive attitude towards their health, and copy them.
10. Make a list of questions (your checklist) you'd like to ask your surgeon before your operation. Make a copy for him/her, too. Pilots refer to their checklists before take-off. Surgeons do, too. And so should you.

11. Smile more, complain less. Complaining or blaming doesn't contribute anything positive to anyone's well-being. It has the opposite effect.
12. Make health awareness your priority. Take full responsibility. After all, it's **your** health.
13. Be grateful. Gratitude is one of life's hidden cures. And so is forgiveness.
14. Cultivate a habit of self-preservation - laughter, being in nature, listening to classical music. Practise the art of contentment.
15. Start asking yourself questions. What am I afraid of? Is this fear helping or hindering my healing?
16. Walk 20 to 30 minutes per day.
17. Cultivate a positive attitude. Leave grudges and jealousy behind. They're toxic.
18. Get regular dental and eye check-ups.

Ghandi once said: *"You must be the change you wish to see in the world"*. He clearly understood that the majority of human beings are afraid of change, afraid to change. We'd rather hold on to what we view as safe and familiar and blame others for any unforeseen circumstances, what we view as 'I don't deserve this'. But change is inevitable. The seasons change, the tides change, and so does the wind direction. Our cells change, and so do our bodies. We even change our minds from time to time. Change can be wonderful, exciting, enlightening.

Taking Responsibility

Patients too need to fulfil their responsibility to themselves. They need to become smart, proactive and scrupulously informed about their bodies and health. With anything short of knowing and understanding they will remain incapacitated. One doesn't have to be in a wheelchair or bedridden to be debilitated. The mere fact that patients know very little about the state of their health renders them such.

I find that men, especially, are more reluctant to 'take charge' of their health. Generally speaking, men tend to say "The doctor or surgeon knows best. Let him get on with it." Some of the men I questioned actually said they "don't need to know. I'm not bothered." Yet, they would be bothered if it was a problem with their car.

Here in the UK there's a compulsory annual health check for vehicles set by the Ministry of Transport to make sure the vehicle in road-worthy called an MOT. If the mechanic finds something wrong he has to fix it; give it a clean bill of health before issuing a certificate. Let's take a quick look at some of the variations of word 'fix': to put right, to renovate, to repair; to put back into working order. And for argument's sake let's say the car represents your body, your health, the mechanic represents you. My question is therefore: are you willing to do the work that's required to keep your body in good working order? Hopefully, the next time you see the sign over the mechanic's shop with the words – body repairs – you will take the necessary action when it comes to your own body.

From questioning some male patients I learned that their macho approach to illness often ceases when suddenly they are struck by crushing chest pain; when, like an electric shock, the pain shoots down their left arm and up the jaw. Then the real fear sets in. "I had a near miss," they'd say. But sometimes it's too late.

My father-in-law, though a chest physician, would put off having the triple heart by-pass he so desperately needed. The thought of cardiac surgery terrified him. He would keep a calm and composed demeanour; he would medicate himself. Sadly, the day came when that course of action was ineffective. After my double valve replacement – some years later – my brother-in-law said his father would have been very proud of me for having such courage.

A female consultant contacted me one day to say: "There's another key area that needs to be urgently addressed: the patient's responsibility for personal health, i.e. prevention of illness, eating well, exercising, and so on.

"Much money in the NHS is spent on treating preventable diseases. It is therefore important for people to focus on not becoming patients at all so that what resources there are, are spent on those who cannot help finding themselves in such a position. Doctors get very frustrated when treating those who decline to take responsibility for something which they can control and manage themselves." What she is referring to here is a change in lifestyle.

The big question is: are patients too reliant on medication? Are doctors too keen to prescribe – repeatedly? Should doctors hand out alternative prescriptions that say: walk more, laugh more; get more sleep; eat less fat, salt, sugar; follow your dreams, even. And what ever happened to a good old chat to get things off one's chest? Would patients benefit more from attending a retreat or workshop? One profound insight I've gained over the years is that people feel better, less insecure, and in some cases less stressful, when they realise that 'they are not alone'. They are not the only ones with deep-seated anger, or have skeletons in their closets, or getting a divorce.

The Consequences of Negative Habits

Other examples of our negative talk could be: "Look what happened to so and so", or, "I'm afraid to get burned again", even, "once bitten, twice shy". If we were insulted or ridiculed for doing something naughty as children, we grow up unconsciously doing our utmost to shun what we think could be a repeat of that emotional pain. Hurt creates fear. Like Frances, the lady who had her tonsils out at age eight. We tell our children to, "mind how you go", or "be careful", indicating that danger is lurking somewhere outside the door. And this is especially so if there has been an accident, incident or murder somewhere, anywhere.

Without exception, all of these negative habits and behaviours can leave us feeling inadequate; cause us to develop a low self-image, lack confidence, or believe that others are better, smarter; therefore, they are more likely to get further in life. Think for a moment of something, or a situation, that is affecting you negatively. Examine it, and see how long you have been dragging it through life. Is it the reason you blame others or situations, get angry or frustrated, drink too much, or over-eat? There is a famous line from the movie Magnolia *"We may be through with the past, but the past is not through with us."*

Unaware of the consequences of that ingrained behaviour, people remain doubtful, suspicious, resentful, even. Fear, this learned, self-inflicted illness, cripples everyone who is afraid of anything. Ignorant of this, people are unable to shed light on the problem because they're too cautious to be curious; too cautious to take a risk, or make a decision for fear of making a mistake, or as some say "making a fool of themselves". In the same way that it is impossible to sew beetroot seeds and harvest sweet peas, it is impossible to sow fear and negativity and reap good health or lasting success. I once heard an American neuro-scientist tell his audience that *"fear shuts down our healing mechanisms"*.

Marie Curie taught us that that which we "fear is only to be understood". At the beginning I mentioned the dark and how it disappears once the light is switched on. It is impossible to run from fear. What we're never taught is that in the end what we fear comes back; it becomes a self-fulfilling prophecy – "be careful what you wish for". Why not ask yourself: how did I create this situation, this illness, and what can **I** do to change it? The fact of the matter is, no one else can eat, sleep, drink or have a blood test for you. So it is crucial, therefore, for you to take full responsibility for the changes you would like to bring about in your life. After all, it is your life. So are you willing to take a risk, be curious? Are you willing to leave blame behind, and open your healing mechanisms by slowly releasing yourself from the 'invisible' prison called fear?

I hope it is clear that fear (consciously or unconsciously) is not a bridge. Being afraid does not give us the results, or the connections, we hope for. It's like standing still while expecting to somehow move forward. From what scientists tell us, it destroys our cells and creates disease. Viewed from that perspective, fear is more of a barricade to happiness and wellbeing in all areas of our life; whether financial health, success, a healthy marriage, physical or emotional wellbeing, or one's healthcare. And it will remain a hindrance until *you* realise that *within you* lies the power to cure it, to overcome it. Let's look at the dictionary's explanation of the word power: the ability to do something; the ability to influence a situation – not necessarily by brute force or bullying!

Why not begin your healing process by speaking out and expressing your feelings about a situation? What you have to say matters.

The Language We Use

Most of us are unaware of the fact that the language we use has consequences, sometimes unfavourable. We can't focus (whether in our thoughts or the words we use) on the bad and expect to get good results outcome.

For example, when a woman discovers she has cancer, people usually say she's going to 'fight' the disease. Is it truly a matter of 'fighting' a disease? Is it 'a battle'? Are we at war with the illness or the disease? This approach to the illness is often compounded by the media: so and so – usually some celebrity – has *beaten* breast cancer. Or, Mr Jones has *lost his battle* against cancer after fighting the disease for X number of months or years. From first-hand experience with my mother, older sister, friends, and from research, cancer patents are so weakened by their treatment and the prospect of dying that 'fighting' doesn't seem to come into it. Scared, what they really want is to know "How much time have I got?"

Since we cannot separate our minds from our bodies, then it is probable that the true battle, the *real cause,* happens internally in the guise of negative thoughts, long-held fears; dissatisfaction with life, deep resentments, guilt, and feelings of frustration, shame, insecurity, anger and lack of gratitude.

What is (silently) eating away at you?

Some people believe their ill-health to be the work of some external force. It's some sort of 'punishment' that one must endure. Others are ashamed that this has happened to them. Why me? They lament. Some patients even end up blaming the medical profession for being unable to 'cure' them; or the government for not providing what they perceive to be a better health service. None of these approaches is an effective remedy. As a matter of fact, they corrode rather than cure. Please take a closer look at what causes stress and what stress causes. What we put out in emotions and thoughts (negative or positive) comes back amplified. Picture a boomerang. No matter how far you throw it, it comes back – with even greater force!

In the end it's about having the courage to confront the illness, the disease, and doing everything in one's power to get well. And that includes finding out more about the problem by asking more questions, gaining more knowledge and then taking positive action.

During my research I came upon something I'd never heard of before called Logotherapy – health through meaning or reason. It is the philosophical practice relating to human responsibility and provides tools for people to handle life's unexpected changes, by asking the question, "How can I deal with this?" as opposed to "Why is this happening to me?"

When I read the serialisation of Philip Gould's (Lord Gould) moving experience of living with cancer in *The Times* newspaper (11-16 July 2011) entitled *The Unfinished Life: An Odyssey of Love and Cancer*, I was deeply inspired. Not only did I learn something more about the disease, but I took heart from his honesty, his sense of humour, his fears, as well as his vulnerability. He never once apportioned blame or asked why me? In essence, he was asking the above question – How can I deal with this?

This is what Tony Blair told his friend Lord Gould when he learned that the cancer had returned two years after a major operation: *"Because the cancer has not finished, it is simply not done with you, it wanted more. You may have changed but not by enough, now you have to go on to a higher spiritual level still. You have to use this recurrence to find your real purpose in life."*

It was obvious from the article that Lord Gould – former Labour party communications aide and an architect of New Labour – had emerged from his three-year ordeal totally transformed. He should be an inspiration to anyone facing such a life-changing/life-threatening illness. He exemplified positivity and hope; even in the face of death.

Finally, it's important to understand that we are the only ones in control of our thoughts, feelings and fears. And when we learn to do that we can ask the relevant questions, absorb the information given and, with the support of family and friends, make the right decisions. Like Lord Gould, (in spite of the fact that he hadn't cured his illness) boldly ask yourself: How can I deal with this?

Illness Doesn't Discriminate

Another thing that's apparent is that illness, no matter what type, is classless; though some people may not see it that way. There is no cultural or social divide, no social status, when it comes to sickness, a disease. Illness doesn't favour the lawyer or doctor over the dustman, or the lady at the supermarket check-out. A heart attack will be the same no matter how rich, no matter how socially deprived the person having it is. And so will be the treatment, whether NHS or private.

Illness, like oxygen, is one of the things in life that makes us all the same. If a patient sitting in a consulting room with his or her doctor or surgeon could view the situation from this perspective, maybe questioning and ultimately learning wouldn't be so difficult. And feelings of intimidation by medical 'authority' that seem to plague patients would slowly diminish.

On the other hand, a great many clinicians and other healthcare professionals are equally anxious about communicating with patients. Imagine how a surgeon feels when he has to inform the relative sitting nervously in the waiting room that the operation hasn't been a success. Or an anaesthetist whose patient doesn't wake up. The same applies to the GP who is looking at your negative test results on the computer screen while you sit before her.

We mustn't forget that doctors are human beings too. They laugh, drink, get angry, some smoke; and, like the rest of us, they make mistakes. They swear too! And from what I've witnessed firsthand, male doctors are not very good patients! And indeed, a few male doctors have told me that they prefer to give injections than to receive them. They admit to being squeamish when it comes to being poked and prodded!

Some people have challenged me on this chapter in my original version. They said: "What about people who can't afford to go to the doctor, or pay for medication?" So, I would like to make my message a bit clearer. We are all human beings, which in itself makes us all the same regardless of our gender, age, social status, religion, education, or culture.

One of my consultants is a man whose credentials and expertise place him at the top of his field. During one of our doctor/patient discussions he told me that they are only four specialists in his area of medicine in the United Kingdom. Not only was I impressed, I felt exceedingly fortunate to be under his care. A couple of years later he told me that he'd had a mini stroke. We jokingly compared notes about having this temporary affliction – his in the right hemisphere of the brain causing his left side to be temporarily paralyzed. And mine, the left, affecting my right arm. We talked about being on Warfarin. This drug, or similar, is prescribed for anyone who has had this experience, or mine (replacement heart valves) – in any part of the world.

I am not referring to affordability, nor am I am insensitive to the fact that those living in dire circumstances and unhealthy conditions can't afford the medication most of us take for granted. The reality is, even doctors and rich people feel pain, have heart attacks; or suffer from Parkinson's disease, even dementia and depression. Some die from cancer or alcohol related diseases – just like anyone else.

In addition to the common cold, to which all of us are vulnerable, we're a collective energy, life force; and this makes us all the same.

Healing From the Inside Out

There are different schools of thought as to why, when, and how we believe and act in the way we do. Some psychologists say that illness starts with our emotions based on our childhood experiences, our mis-guided beliefs, our disappointments and expectations. While modern-day researchers are convinced it begins in the mind, with our thoughts. While some spiritual doctrines maintain it is all cause and effect: what we think, say or do produces corresponding effects or consequences. They tell us that we can become masters of our minds. Perhaps it's all of the above. Ignorant of this, we allow our minds to master us.

As a schoolteacher, Joyce – the patient I spoke of earlier – appreciated my idea of homework! It went something like this: "Get a writing-pad and write your feelings down. Every day, several times a day, if necessary. Ask yourself questions. Rehearse them to yourself. Be honest. It's for your eyes only – so go crazy! You can destroy what you've written afterwards if you wish. This action will, in the end, help you make the decision that is right for you and your family. But the decision is yours only. Others will give an opinion, but ultimately, you will have to follow your heart."

We talked about our conditioning and how we somehow expect others to read our minds, dissect our thoughts and make our decisions for us. They don't have crystal balls. Dr Johnson gave her his professional opinion. In the end, it was up to Joyce. As I was about to leave the ward a few hours later she said, "I've been lying here thinking about what you said. I've more or less made a decision, but will give it some more thought and talk it through with my husband."

She smiled. I winked. "The hospital should hire you," she said.

An equally powerful method I mentioned to Joyce is to sit quietly, or walk slowly, in nature – alone. It is called self-preservation, being kind to you. This is something we're rarely, if ever, taught.

I read an interesting article in *The New York Times* about a new wave of research that urges self-compassion. According to Dr Kristin Neff, an associate professor of human development at the University of Texas at Austin, *"I found in my research that the biggest reason people aren't more self-compassionate is that they are afraid they'll become self-indulgent. They believe self-criticism is what keeps them in line. Most people have gotten it wrong, because our culture says being hard on yourself is the way to be."*

I interviewed a former corporate high-flyer, a woman in late her fifties, who'd had a severe stroke four years earlier that left her virtually paralysed from the waist down and with limited movement in her arms. I was encouraged by her philosophical approach.

"In the end I had to see it as a blessing, a wake-up call," she told me.

"Why was it a wake-up call?"

"Because, ultimately, what I had to come to terms with was not the stroke, but me. It was a huge challenge. I was very angry. Absolutely furious. As someone who was highly competitive and fiercely independent, reduced to being housebound, physically helpless and dependent, was very difficult for me. I wanted to know why me.

"But over time it caused me to take a long hard look at my life, my values, and my relationships. It stopped me in my tracks. Literally! Thankfully, I still have my wits about me," she laughed.

"When I was in the corporate world my whole life revolved around money, things, more, more, more; the bigger the better. I used to believe that having things made me important, and a better person. It was how I identified myself. It took me a couple of years to see that there was more to me than that. It was all superficial. Now less is more. One day I gave everything away. It liberated me. I now appreciate the simple things in life, like watching the birds flitter from tree to tree. I've even come to recognise different species. And, believe it or not, rain and grey skies are no longer an issue."

I said, "Can you tell me one thing you wish you could do?"

"You may not believe this, but it's something so simple. One day I was sitting here just gazing at the floor. I just stared. I stared wondering what it would be like to sit on that floor and get up again....on my own. We take those little things for granted."

Illness and psychological distress are facts of life, as are anxiety, pain, sorrow, aging and ultimately, death. It would be naive of us to believe otherwise. The above experience illustrates the fact that we can use the illness positively and transform our lives. I've encountered a number of terminally ill people who have said, "I'm okay with dying. I've left everything in order." They had transformed their fears into something healing; even if the illness itself hadn't healed.

Prevention is Better than Cure

"The doctor of the future will give no medicine, but will interest her or his patients in the care of the human frame, in a proper diet, and in the cause and prevention of disease". - Thomas Edison (1847 - 1931)

Illness begins in the stomach, some health experts warn us. They also remind us that healing does, too. Psychologists and spiritual leaders across the globe say that our conditioning and beliefs, negative or positive, play a vital role in our wellbeing, too. Our minds and bodies are inseparable. Sometime ago I had access to a DVD, *Hungry for Change – Your Health is in Your Hands*. As I watched the number of health and fitness experts share some potent advice, I was reminded that we are not eating proper food anymore. One contributor said that "we are eating food-like products." We're all seduced by the tantalising looks and smells of food, aromas that instinctively make us feel hungry, even if we're not. Like a bakery with attractive looking donuts and cupcakes piled high with an array of coloured icing, as well as freshly baked loaves of bread.

A good old-fashioned loaf of bread contains four ingredients: flour, water, yeast and salt. Shockingly, if you check the ingredients listed on the packaging of a loaf wrapped in plastic you will see a staggering number of ingredients. In addition to the above ingredients there are caramelised sugar, butter, oil, fermented wheat flour, vegetable fat, wheat protein, emulsifiers, flour treatment agent, and a couple of E's. The package says that this loaf is naturally rich in wholegrain goodness for a healthy heart! But is this true?

According to Dr Christiane Northrup MD, an American Obstetrician/Gynaecologist, "Sugar is the cocaine of the food industry. There is a lot of food around, but it's the wrong kind. Sugar is a drug – just like alcohol." She then went on to say, "You might as well be rolling up your kids' sleeves and putting in heroin, because it's the same." If this is not an eye-opener, I don't know what is. On one of Dr Northup's weekly online radio shows she urged mothers to walk down the cereal aisles in the supermarket and check the labels. She urged her listeners to note the amount of sugar (and salt) they are pumping into their children's diet at the beginning of their day.

Most ready meals are high in calories, but low in nutrition. There is a worldwide epidemic in the form of diabetes. Some healthcare professionals have described this as a time bomb waiting to go off. What we eat, drink and think determines our health. So does our indoor, couch potato lifestyle. I watched an interesting and informative BBC Horizon programme, *The Truth about Exercise,* presented by Michael Mosley, a trained doctor, who tested the effectiveness of different types of exercises. With a history of diabetes, he wanted to do everything possible to combat the disease. In the end he found the exercise that suited him best. According to the experts on the programme, exercise is not a one-size-fits-all solution. Mosley's last words were "the chair is a killer". Doesn't that make you want to get up and do some form of movement for at least thirty minutes a day?

From time to time some people find themselves with unexplained symptoms. They rush to the doctor who in turn writes a prescription. Could it be that these symptoms are a result of their diet? I've been watching a number of programmes on health as part of my ongoing education. What is obvious is that we are ultimately responsible for our health. Diet plays a huge part. In one, a doctor of natural medicine said that most food labels are misleading.

Nutritional experts tell us that our 'healthy options' may not be so healthy after all. They usually single out foods labelled: fat free, low fat, healthy option, low calorie, low sodium, zero calories and more. But what preserves these foods? White sugar is a pharmaceutical product. Even the fruits in some muffins are not natural fruit, but have been scientifically modified.

Under British imperialism, merchants shipped sugar to the UK, refined and processed it on a colossal scale and then resold it to the countries that had produced it in the first place in the form of white sugar. Now an import, it was more expensive than the original product. Naively, we believed "it must be better for us because it came from England". Sugar cane was, and remains, a 'cash crop'. About twenty years ago, we knew a

City trader whose bonuses from the sale of sugar made him the wealthiest person I knew.

Pure cane sugar, or evaporated cane juice, as it is also known, comes in a variety of textures and colours such as Demerara or Muscovado. And there is molasses, a thick black sticky substance slightly bitter in taste. Most people living in sugar producing countries chew the fresh sugar cane. It's part of the culture. My memory of people harvesting the crop on the plantations when I was a girl is of white teeth 'flossed' by the abrasiveness of the cane husks while chewing. I know this from personal experience!

Dr Northrup said in a programme, *"Premature death is caused by too much sugar, alcohol and smoking."* A BBC report online read, *"Deaths from liver disease in England have reached record levels, rising by 25% in less than a decade, according to new NHS figures. Heavy drinking, obesity and hepatitis are believed to be behind the rise."*

Since then (14.08.2012) the BBC reported some frightening revelations: *The number of prescriptions for treating diabetes in England has topped 40 million, figures show. This is a 50% rise in six years and a 6.1% (2.3m) rise on the number of items prescribed in 2010-11, data from the Health and Social Care Information Centre reveals. In England, 2.5m people have been diagnosed with diabetes and the number is expected to reach 4.2m by 2025.*

History shows that it was the British merchants who were responsible for feeding the world sugar. Now, centuries later, the likes of Jamie Oliver and other chefs are trying to redress what their ancestors had done by educating the world to the health hazards of eating too much sugar, one of the commodities that made their country the richest in the world.

In the film *Hungry for Change,* Jamie showed an audience the amount of refined sugar they are feeding their children daily, particularly with flavoured milk drinks. He produced a wheelbarrow full of refined sugar cubes and told mothers that that's the amount of sugar their children will have consumed by the time the leave primary school. Along with this jaw-dropping information, I learned that "unhealthy food kills more people per year than all drugs combined, because they are loaded with sugar and unhealthy fats." A nutritionist said, "Our bodies do not process man-made foods. Most of what we eat is unhealthy bulk. Therefore, we're over-fed and under-nourished." The purpose of these hard-hitting facts is to educate us to make better choices.

In addition to the sugars there are take-away curries, fish and chips, kebabs, along with the ready meals all containing large amounts of unhealthy carbohydrates and fats – bad cholesterol. There is no shortage of butchers selling fatty meats like pork belly carved into two inch strips and neatly displayed in the window. It is one of the cheapest cuts of meat. It is also all fat. I've watched some celebrity chefs glorify pork belly as they fry it off in the pan. Celebrity chefs and cookery programmes are equally guilty of glamourising their high fat, sugar and salt recipes. Most shamefully, they fry a lot. My question is: Whatever happened to 'an apple a day'?

Throughout these pages I've touched upon the fact that we, the patients, the consumers, are the power behind our health, even if we don't believe it. So why don't we believe this? Could it be because we were taught that doctors are the ones in control? People believe that because doctors are the ones who studied the human anatomy, its diseases and complexities, and just about everything that can go wrong with the human body and how to diagnose and treat symptoms, then write prescriptions and send us for blood tests, they know everything. They don't. My ongoing research tells me that people still believe they, the patients, are powerless.

But the truth of the matter is, doctors do not take us to the supermarket, and they do not write the shopping lists. They can't tell you how to respond to the emotional experience you might be having. They cannot tell you how to think, what to say, or whether or not you should stop hating your mother or sister for something that happened years ago. These are some of the deeply painful wounds – unexplained aches and pains – that doctors are unable to cure. Because until you heal your past negative situations, wounds in the guise of shame, grudges, fear, anger, feelings of inadequacy, food addiction, smoking, etc, you will continue to bleed. And no amount of vitamin K (used to clot blood) will stop the bleeding. It doesn't matter how tightly the doctor may wrap the bandage, he/she will never be able to contain the flow of your negative emotions or the constant flow of dissatisfaction with your life.

Doctors cannot predict your happiness or write a prescription for your low self-esteem, or its opposite, confidence. Indeed, doctors themselves are stricken with some of the same psychological and emotional illnesses. Don't forget that they were taught some of the same life-lessons. They're human, too! I heard a retired general practitioner say in a talk he was giving that he'd had more than 5,000 encounters with patients per year. He went on to describe its negative effects on his life. Do we ever wonder how doctors cope? Below is an extract from a letter sent to me by a woman with whom I'd had a conversation as we walked in our local park about health:

"My darling sister was a doctor, a GP. She was so entrenched in her work that she neglected to look after her own health. She knew very little about healthy eating, or how integral food is to a healthy body. We had many discussions over the years and invariably ended up by agreeing to disagree on our different approaches to healthcare: she from the conventional medical standpoint and I from the naturopathic or holistic. My sister developed diabetes and cancer. I'm not saying that her dietary lifestyle was the direct cause of her health problems and subsequent death. She had deeply buried emotional issues, too, which she never processed."

Here are a few questions I'd encourage you to ask yourself:
- What is missing in my life? What am I aching (longing) for?
- What's eating me? And is over-eating the answer?
- What unfinished business from my past am I still humping around?
- Why am I still holding that grudge, that anger, that shame or that guilt?
- Am I in denial? What am I seeing but pretend I'm not seeing?
- What emotional needs or void am I trying to 'comfort' or 'fill'?
- Am I trying to eat and drink my way to the grave hoping to achieve some satisfaction?
- What is causing my stress?

How hungry are you for change, for a healthier lifestyle? Equally important, what positive lessons are you teaching your children about health, about prevention?

Empathy

Please do not think for one moment that I am being insensitive to the plight of the less well off. Nor am I judging or criticizing the single mother living on the housing estate with a number of mouths to feed. I have deep respect for the elderly as I was raised by grandparents and taught from a very early age that the elderly are to be respected, almost revered, and not mocked or harassed. In my opinion a community without the elderly is a mere shell with no depth or history; it is soulless.

There are many elderly men and women who are extremely inspirational. They are fit and healthy and have a very simple diet. They have a sense of humour; they're satisfied with life, no matter how it may look to the outside world. I've found this to be true more so amongst the poor and less well off. Likewise, there are many elderly people who are living on their own with very little help. What kind of society do we live in where the community doesn't feel a sense of responsibility for its elders?

Speaking of single mothers, I am the second of eight children, born to a teenage mother. Between us we have five fathers, all of whom walked away. There was little or no financial assistance. Mothers like mine did menial jobs and did without luxuries in order to feed their children. We had to make do with the modest resources available. We ate the cheapest cuts of meat, which were basically fat. Luckily, there was no shortage of fresh fish, a favourite, fried in lard.

They bartered with the country women who brought their freshly harvested produce to market. In some cases money was never exchanged. We raised chickens and pigs in the backyard – where the children played! And if the children got sick and the doctor was called, he had to be paid. His services were considered private. Whereas, hospital treatment was free. Now, as I go about my daily life, I observe young mothers feeding their offspring in more or less the same way. But there is one stark difference: today's mothers 'treat' themselves and their children to 'luxuries' - hair and nail extensions, numerous pairs of shoes, and 'treats' from the supermarkets.

When I arrived in New York in 1970 I was excited by the vast array of food and portion sizes. So I ate massive steaks, hamburgers, piled high pastrami sandwiches, finger lickin' good fried chicken, and devoured endless pizzas. At that time I was unaware of the salt, sugar, fat and preservatives in foods. Or that I was feeding my body an untold number of calories, but very little nutrition. Yes, I do know what it's like to use food as a means to comfort oneself.

And even after I arrived in London, got married and lived a more middle-class lifestyle, I would be enticed by some very unhealthy foods. And, as a trained cordon bleu cook with a fledgling catering business, I would prepare tantalizingly delicious and beautifully presented food, not dissimilar to that of today's TV chefs.

Not surprisingly, there is always a reason why we become seduced by 'instant' meals, apart from the fact that most of them are moreish! Mine was my busy hospital schedule with my daughter, and when in 1995 I learned I had a cardiac problem, I sought the professional advice of a dietician. This caused me to look more closely at the way we were eating as a family. Though there was not too much unhealthy food, still, I had to apply the discipline across the board.

After my cardiac surgery I brought exercise back into my daily schedule. What has continued to be my major driving force is my family history of type 2 diabetes. I would rather give up certain foods, exercise regularly, than take medication. We always have to let go of something, even if it's something we like. Years ago we didn't know any better. The idea of 'learning something about your health condition' was difficult, if not impossible. The 'information highway' was a mere dirt track. At that time only those in the medical professional were privy to, or understood, medical information. What I'm about to say may shock you: doctors spend an average of six years in medical training. During that time very little time was focused on nutrition. I believe that has, or is, changing somewhat.

The importance of patient education can't be stressed enough. Today, more than any other time in history we have the means to avoid many illnesses by using the information readily available to us. We have the internet; with a click of the mouse we can order from any online bookstore. Our libraries are stacked, and there are a number of medical journals available in bookshops and newsagents. Even television channels are getting in on the act as doctors become presenters, giving us living examples of anything from diabetes to heart disease, from super sized to super skinny.

I've developed a ferocious appetite for health education. And I would encourage you to do the same. This knowledge keeps me disciplined as far as my diet, exercise and overall health are concerned. Yes, I sometimes lapse. Occasionally, I treat myself to small amounts of the foods I enjoy, like Basmati rice, pasta and potatoes; foods that quickly spike the blood sugar levels, especially when eaten in large quantities. I still enjoy the occasional piece of chocolate. Less is more. Being informed has great advantages. It also helps to build confidence.

So what is the answer to good health? In a word: education, action. The experts say that we should read the labels, know what we're buying. And not be fooled by fancy labelling. Some American doctors are telling their patients that it's not about the pill they're taking, but chiefly, about the food they're eating. Although they say prescription medication has its place, it saves lives. But in their expert opinion, it's what we put in to our stomachs that will kill or cure us.

We're encouraged to eat more fresh, and if possible, organic fruits and vegetables, healthy fats and healthy carbohydrates – the kind that is released slowly into the bloodstream. What happened to good old home-cooked meals? Fresh food doesn't have to be as expensive as people imagine. Is there a farmers' market near you? How about allotments? There are land-share schemes in certain parts of the country. More and more people are growing their vegetables in plant pots. Buying from the supermarkets is only one option. There are many recipes with ideas for deliciously wholesome and inexpensive meals. You just have to be willing to change, to try something new; make good health your priority. The reality is, you are going to have to pay in some way, either with your purse or your health. The choice is yours. Your health is in your hands. It begins with YOU.

Is your health a priority? If not, why not? We were taught moral values, but what about 'values in healthcare'? Again, think about the messages you are sending your children.

Healthcare v Medical Care

I've repeatedly said that healthcare begins with the individual. It is the patient who is solely responsible for his/her health, not the government. There are, of course, exceptions. Namely, those sections of society where people caring for themselves is extremely complex, and sometimes virtually impossible: the dependent elderly, the terminally ill (especially those who have no one to care for them), the disabled, the homeless, and those suffering from mental illness. Not everyone is capable of applying the concept of Self-Responsibility. Healthcare also begins with the mother who trains her child's palate. Healthcare begins with a society that upholds moral values. A healthy society thrives when its people are tolerant; when there is respect and compassion for the elderly, the list is endless.

Government cannot be held responsible for what people are not providing for themselves. We are solely responsible for the thoughts we think, the words we utter, the actions we take – consciously or unconsciously, negative or positive. Social care (our contribution to society), reaching out to others, irrespective of our circumstances, should play a large part in our healthcare. It can be therapeutic, and immensely healing.

There is another vital component to healthcare – spiritual healing. Spiritual teachers throughout the ages have used, and indeed taught, that love, gratitude, silence, peace, respect, laughter, compassion, and humility, are some of the healthy ways to nourish the soul, heal the body, and exercise the mind. Joy, for example, is not a buzzword in today's society. People prefer to be miserable, complain endlessly about what is not working, what they haven't got; or what the politicians are not doing. They worry. Joy is healing; it unbinds the heart from the restrictions we place on it. In the words of the Scottish novelist Robert Louis Stevenson (1850-1894) – *"Find out where joy resides, and give it a voice far beyond singing. For to miss joy is to miss all."*

The other component to health, for which government is responsible, is the provision of medical care, the National Health Service: surgery, diagnosing congenital diseases, cancer or any other disease, fractured bones, strokes, the treatment of infected blood, cardiology, medical research, and so on. These conditions are best dealt with by those who are uniquely qualified, and employed, to 'sort it out': doctors, surgeons, scientists, and other specialists in their field of medicine.

As patients, it is wise to seek the advice of, and work in partnership with, those professionals. Some experts believe this teamwork, this patient/doctor relationship, to be an effective prescription for a better understanding of one's medical condition. The government provides leaflets covering every procedure a patient is about to undergo, or illness they may have, and there is one suggesting questions patients should ask their doctors.

This information is available in every hospital waiting room, on the wards, in every GP surgery and in clinics. They are available to help patients and their families learn something about their condition and make informed decisions. My ongoing research suggests that very few take the time to read this literature. It is a pity because understanding is a powerful tool. Remember, there is nothing blissful about ignorance. So what will it take to educate patients? What will it take to 'create a thirst'?

There is something else the government provides that is largely overlooked, not necessarily appreciated: screening programmes. I received this letter dated 29 May 2012 whose contents made me feel 'taken care of': *"This is an invitation to take part in the NHS Bowel Cancer Screening Programme. The programme aims to detect bowel cancer early, when successful treatment and cure is more likely. Screening is offered every two years to people aged 60-69 who are registered with a GP in England. We are starting to extend this screening age range, so if you are aged 70-74; you are being invited as part of this process."* Similarly, appointments are automatically made for breast and prostate screening. Who foots the bill?

In the end, as users of the service, we have to open our eyes to the fact that the NHS is like a large corporation with a CEO (chief executive officer) at the helm; in this case it's the government, the minister for health. Like any business, accounts have to be balanced; financial decisions have to be made. Sometimes these decisions are harsh and unpopular. We also have to understand that when the health service came about there weren't as many people using its services; not as many illnesses; it wasn't hi-tech, all of which are expensive.

People often say "I pay in to the system". Yes we do make a monetary contribution, but this also goes towards one's state pension. So can our contributions, alone, *really* cover the cost of running our health service? Does the amount each person contributes even cover the financial worth of several GP and hospital visits? What about having an operation or expensive tests and on-going treatment? Because we contribute does it give us the right to waste it? A number of NHS managerial staff told me that unthinkable millions of pounds are wasted each year by patients. Missed appointments and unused drugs are the main areas of waste. Unaware of the price tag and their wastage, patients point their fingers at the government, anyone but themselves. How lucrative is your monetary contribution? Perhaps it would be a good idea if patients were made aware of what their treatment costs. What do you think?

Investing in Patients

America's First Lady, Michelle Obama, has been fronting a campaign to get supermarkets and small grocers across the US to make fresh, wholesome food more available and affordable to the less well off. She also wants to see more farmers markets. She has also been encouraging families to grow their own.

Mrs Obama, along with Britain's Jamie Oliver, both proponents of healthy eating, are on a mission to stem the tide of junk food and childhood obesity plaguing the US and Britain today. Speaking with equal determination, they both believe it's worth the investment, and that this investment will reap dividends in the future.

In a White House speech, *Bringing Healthy, Affordable Food to Underserved Communities*, Mrs Obama pleaded with Americans to stop the habit of fast foods and poor nutrition that have been handed down over the generations. To reinforce her message, she urged them to cultivate the habit of eating more fresh fruit and vegetables, of choosing the healthy option, as well as some form of daily exercise. It is a life-saving investment.

In Britain today there are supermarkets across the land offering cheap deals, healthy and not so healthy. Yet if you look at what's in the trolleys at the checkout they're not filled with healthy options, most of them, but are piled high with ready meals with high fat, salt and sugar content, soft drinks full of E's and other preservatives. Choosing the healthy option has yet to become a habit.

This is not to suggest that people shouldn't have the occasional treat, chocolate, ice cream, cake, pizzas, chips or the odd piece of fried chicken. We all know it can be finger lickin' good! The reformers are referring to unhealthy eating habits.

Let's look at the meaning of the word 'habit': a tendency to act in a particular way; mental disposition or attitude. In short, something we do consistently through our thoughts, words and actions, negative or positive, consciously or subconsciously. Often we hear people say they did this or that without noticing, without realising.

To quote Warren Buffett, the American industrialist and philanthropist," *Habits are too light to be felt until they are too heavy to be broken."* Because habits are 'learned behaviours', they become part of the pattern one follows. Therefore breaking negative habits, the habits that cause us the most pain and dissatisfaction, requires tremendous effort and commitment. But it is possible to re-educate ourselves, to re-train our minds.

Mrs Obama's message was clear. Wellness now halts preventable illness in the future. However, for this to be effective greater access to information is needed. I heard an empowered American patient say, "*Patients are the most underutilised resource in any healthcare system."* He ended his impassioned talk by saying, "*Let patients help."* In other words – encourage patients to help themselves.

Some would argue the point the retired doctor made about curiosity. They would argue that governments cannot dictate whether or not a patient should get involved in his or her health issues. This is true. Springing to mind is another old adage: *You can take a horse to the water, but you can't make it drink.* The concept of patient education could open minds and create a thirst. However, in order for this to happen, patients will have to look inside and see how they are (unknowingly) creating the fear, the denial; see how they are following some backward ideas; ideas and beliefs that make them sick.

Healthcare Costs

In other parts of the world patients have to pay for their medical treatment if they don't have health insurance. In Switzerland, for example, it is compulsory that every citizen has a minimum of £500 worth of private medical insurance. And in most cases, a Swiss national told me, the excess is £1,000. Therefore, if the costs are less, the patient has to pay.

An American woman living in London told me that a few years ago she returned to New York and took ill while she was there. "They charged me a staggering $10,000 for some tests and an overnight stay in hospital. Then, before I'd sorted it out with my insurance provider, I received threatening phone calls for payment." I sat open-mouthed. "And yes," she added, "every hospital in America has a collections department, just like the banks. And they will hound you until the balance is zero. In the States, as you know, hospitals are big business. It probably costs about $15,000 now," she said. We sat praising the British healthcare system.

In some EU countries such as France, healthcare is contributions-based. This simply means that people are not automatically entitled to healthcare, although all emergency cases have to be treated. Patients have to have health insurance to cover the percentage not reimbursed by the government. Those on very low incomes are entitled to free healthcare. An American who doesn't have private health insurance dreads having a medical emergency. Those without healthcare insurance aren't a priority – no matter how critical their condition. Even with President Obama's 'affordable' Healthcare Bill those I've questioned said that for them, it is still unaffordable.

Here are a couple of examples of private patients' costs in the UK in 2012-2013. A hip replacement at one of the UK's leading orthopaedic hospitals costs approximately £14,000. For a heart valve replacement carried out privately at a specialist hospital like the Royal Brompton, a deposit of between £30,000 - £40,000 is required; and £20,000 for a by-pass surgery. There is an additional charge for extra day(s) in intensive care. In the US the cost for this operation is significantly higher. In India, however, the cost is considerably lower.

According to some internet sites medical tourism is on the increase. A patient who doesn't want to wait his turn on an NHS waiting list can have his operation carried out in Asia or the Far East, and for considerably less than it would cost to go the private route in the UK.

But how much do you know about the surgeon who will be performing your operation abroad, or the cleanliness of the hospital where it will be carried out? What if something goes wrong, who will be held responsible? How will you go about filing a complaint? This is not to suggest that the hospital in Singapore or India is worse than its NHS counterpart in Essex or Manchester. On the contrary, there may be better facilities, cleaner wards, less waste. My point is: healthcare is expensive.

In 2004 I was in Barbados. Because I am on Warfarin my blood has to be checked regularly. It would cost me around £15 each time. Sitting next to me in the waiting room one morning was an elderly lady who walked aided with a cane. Retrieving something out of her bosom, she un-wrapped it and slowly, counted out 185 Barbadian dollars (approximately £65) in anticipation of being called to the cashier's window.

Studying her face as she counted the money made me smile. I asked her if she always paid for her blood tests. Smiling softly, she said in a heavy Bajan accent, "Yes, darling. I get a slight discount, but I still have to pay. Every time I count the money, I feel **so** grateful that I have it. Praise God."

"But you're a pensioner," I said, dismayed.

"Don't matter, darling, I still got to pay. I put aside a little something every week."

She was eighty-six. I didn't get the impression that this elder felt like a victim of her circumstances, or the system. She wasn't blaming the government. On the contrary, her attitude was one of contentment and grace. How many NHS patients have such an attitude? From what I've witnessed in hospital waiting rooms over the past twenty-something years I'd say not many.

And what about those living in war-torn countries? Those whose children aren't vaccinated, or referred to a specialist hospital as a matter of course; whose people die from diseases and conditions that we won't ever catch, or that could be easily treated if they had the resources. They would be more than grateful for a two-hour wait in a casualty department. They'd be grateful for the medication and equipment we waste in Britain. Instead, they mostly rely on faith, hope and aid.

About five years ago, a phlebotomist (someone trained to draw blood from a person) told me of a family in her native Ghana. That day I was her last patient, so we chatted more than usual.

"A family brought their 10-year-old daughter to the hospital where I was working. She was always tired and would go blue sometimes. Finally, she was refusing food. They tried everything from natural remedies to witch doctors but when it became clear that she was in the 'danger zone', the father drove for several hours to get medical help. She was diagnosed with a congenital heart problem that she had had from birth. One of her heart valves had to be operated on as a matter of urgency. But the family needed the money to pay for the surgery and aftercare.

"So the father went back to their village and sold everything they had – the livestock, the chickens, even the land that had been handed down from his father and grandfather. The operation was a success. Everyone was happy! But then there was a huge problem. The girl needed Warfarin and it had to be bought. There was no money left; and no more means of getting any. So she died."

I have no idea how much Warfarin and other drugs are disposed of because of a best before date determined by the drug companies.

During an online radio interview the other day (July 2012), an American cardiologist said that he was not only distressed, but appalled by the fact that millions of Americans were without health insurance because they can't afford it. He expressed his deep concerns for his son who was left severely disabled after a car accident. "Always on my mind," the doctor said, "is the fact that we won't be able to afford his healthcare forever. And that hurts."

I was introduced to a Canadian woman in her mid-fifties in 2010 because of our common experience of mothering children with disabilities. She took me to the bedroom to meet her severely disabled six-foot-something son who required round-the-clock care. He responded by smiling and shaking his head. He would grunt and twitch now and again. Like my daughter, his mouth never closed. After ten years in London the family had to leave because her husband had been posted back to Canada. "Sadly, the time has come for us to pack up and leave," she said. "Although we are middle-class and my husband earns a decent salary, we won't be able to afford the staggering Can. $250,000.00 (approximately £160,000.00) it will cost us annually for his care. Here in the UK people don't realise what a great service the NHS provides." Imagine for a moment having to find that whopping sum every year to pay for your child's or spouse's medical and social care.

Unlike these parents, I was more concerned about who would care for my daughter if something happened to me, rather than the provision of her care. And the Canadian mother was right; our country provides a health service – irrespective of cuts or other political issues – that should be highly valued by its users. It is one of the great things about Britain.

Do you ever stop and think of the monetary value of your care? Would it make a difference if you knew the cost of every GP visit, or hospital procedure?

Why It's Good to Talk

"This is slavery, not to speak one's thoughts." Euripides, *the Phoenician Women*

It is possible that when patients stop to consider that doctors are also human and not perfect they will no longer view them as superior. I experienced this when my father-in-law told me that one of his sons had had Down's syndrome. His deeply held 'secret' had been a heavy burden; one he could no longer carry.

First of all, most of us are of the belief that doctors are so powerful there isn't anything they can't do, or don't know. Some doctors find it equally difficult to speak their minds, or ask questions. But lack of communication (failure to speak up and speak out) can sometimes have harmful consequences. We are, in effect, enslaved by the lie, which may not be obvious.

I've decided to share (in part) an extract from a chapter in my book *Raising Tiffany – Portrait of a Special Girl,* in which I tell the experience I had as my father-in-law and I sat in the children's waiting room at St. Thomas's Hospital one morning. Looking at Tiffany, approaching three, as she sat observing the other children at play, he turned to me and said:

"There is something I must share with you." He took a deep breath. "Oliver was a Mongol. I suppose that's not politically correct these days," he added.

Perplexed, I asked, "Oliver who?"

"My Oliver," he said, still looking in Tiffany's direction.

I sat open-mouthed. I knew of Oliver, of course. He was their third child who died at age four; and before my ex, had even been conceived. And when I was pregnant with my Oliver, my mother-in-law said how pleased she was that I'd chosen the name if the baby was a boy.

I finally asked him if my husband knew.

"No," Hugh said in an almost inaudible tone, never taking his eyes off his granddaughter.

"No? None of your children know about this?" My eyes popped in disbelief.

He finally turned in me. Clearly embarrassed, he said that only the two older children knew. This puts a different slant on 'family secrets'; not only hiding things from the outside world, but from our loved ones. It seems that human beings prefer to suffer in silence. So where in our bodies does this negative energy reside?

I sat wondering. I wasn't sure if I was gutted, shocked, disappointed, or angry. Perhaps all of the above. We sat in silence until Tiffany's name was called.

"Tiffany exhibits some Down's syndrome characteristics, but she is not Down's." These had been the words of the consultant geneticist at the Great Ormond Street Hospital, as he had studied the results of the analysis of her chromosomes a few months earlier.

Our conversation continued once we'd arrived back at the flat.

"Over forty years have gone by and this is the very first time I'm admitting my failure," his soft voice disclosed.

"But you're a doctor. I don't understand."

"You see Debbie that was probably the biggest reason why, because *I am* a doctor. I am someone who is supposed to cure people; at least diagnose their symptoms accurately. I wasn't able to do so when it came to my own son." Hugh wiped his brow. "As doctors, we are looked upon by society as 'miracle workers'. It is simply awful when one can't perform a miracle on one's own child."

He took a deep breath. "Debbie," he said, tapping his chest, "whilst sitting in the clinic watching Tiffany a short while ago, something pierced my heart. I realised then, that I had to tell you. You had to know." He wiped his spectacles. I sat silently not knowing what to say or how to handle the bomb that had just landed in my lap.

That was the moment I took doctors off the pedestals. The pedestals most people in society have placed them on. Our belief that doctors are 'God's gift to man' not only makes us feel insecure in their presence, but it's a heavy burden to them as well. That morning I sat looking at a man; a father whose five children saw him vulnerable to long bouts of depression.

Be that as it may, my father-in-law was a respectable human being, someone I was incredibly fond of who had trusted me on this and other occasions with things that had sat in his heart for years. Like the time he told me that he was not a good father, but a good provider; one who openly admitted to being emotionally disconnected from his family.

Hugh, with sadness in his eyes went on to say, "So much pressure is put on the medical profession. Somehow, and for some strange reason, we're not expected to lead our lives like ordinary people. That pressure Debbie, was unnatural, and at times, unbearable. At least it was for me."

"And perhaps it still is," I added.

"Perhaps it still is," Hugh replied. His gaze fixed on the open window.

He died some months later.

We sometimes talk about getting things off our chests, but don't necessarily know why we need to do so; or indeed, the consequences of such action. Years ago British Telecom had a slogan 'It's good to talk'. And in this ad people were doing just that – talking. Today more than ever, people are talking; even a toddler has a mobile phone! But I'm not referring to gossip or mindless chit-chat, but having the courage to be vulnerable; the courage to open the door, unearth **your** skeletons and air them.

We all have deeply buried secrets in some form or another: anger, long-held grudges, something you felt terribly ashamed of and tried to forget. Yet, something or someone sparked the memory or pushed your buttons reminding you that haven't dealt with it, haven't cleared the air, and haven't forgiven that person, or indeed yourself. I'd encourage you to listen closely to these 'messages'. Equally important, don't let what others think, or how you think they will judge you, stop you.

The big question is, what if these 'hidden secrets', these 'difficult conversations', the 'dirty linen' we were taught not to air in public, are causing some of your ailments, like stress and depression, and more – the illnesses not even the most experienced doctors can halt, no matter how much medication they prescribe.

I've heard modern-day thinkers and psychologists say that holding on to these toxic emotions (skeletons) is based on what we were taught by our society. These experts believe that it is not necessarily our genes that cause illnesses and diseases, but the beliefs we've inherited. *(I've recommend a number of books at the back for your information).*

Are you willing to be vulnerable? Are you ready to speak up and speak out? Who will you talk to? And if you're the listener, will you listen with compassion or will you judge and interrupt with your opinion? By the way, if you find an effective way that works for you, why not share it with others. Shout it from the rooftop! This may not be a very British way to behave, but to heck with tradition – shout! Rudyard Kipling once said: *"Words are, of course, the most powerful drug used by mankind."*

It was obvious that my father-in-law, whose education and middle-class beliefs had made it difficult for him to talk, had finally found a reason to speak up, speak out. On that sunny morning boundaries were crossed. Hugh broke with tradition. Or, as the English would say, he did the 'proper' thing.

He also taught me something else I've been applying to my life since that day in 1987: "Stand your ground for what you believe to be right." He knew there was no quick fix, or a cure for Tiffany's condition. Fully aware of my journey ahead, and the challenges I would encounter as I went from hospital to hospital with his granddaughter, he decided to 'train' me. Years after his passing I used his invaluable guidance to challenge an eye surgeon. I vehemently questioned his decision to put my daughter under general anaesthetic; a procedure that could have had disastrous consequences. But, I had to know the facts. In the end, I not only demanded an apology from the surgeon, but told him he would never touch Tiffany again.

Thanks to Hugh I've learned that curiosity is the key to understanding, the key to self-empowerment. I've since recognised this experience as a gift from him, one I'm sharing with you.

Gratitude – A Potent Remedy

Gratitude is an exceedingly powerful and effective method of healing both the mind and body. And sometimes the benefits are very subtle, almost invisible. The healing I'm referring to here is the healing of attitude, the healing of our fear-driven lives; healing from the inside out. A number of people have cured their illnesses because they believed it was possible to do so by recognising and letting go of their dissatisfaction, deeply held resentments, anger, and so on. With a new outlook, they began to feel grateful for everything in their lives – including the disease. Like Anne in the chapter *Those Who Inspired Me* who was awaiting a heart donor. Or indeed, the young cystic fibrosis patient reminded us of the value in being able to inhale oxygen naturally.

Because of their self-discovery a new world, a refreshing outlook on life appeared. They experienced more joy, thanked their doctors, expressed gratitude to the nurses and to their carers. They looked at the trees and flowers with appreciation for life. Not all healing comes via a doctor's prescription pad.

More and more doctors – in America and Britain – are prescribing meditation, being in nature, or being quiet for at least thirty minutes daily, as alternatives to prescription drugs to treat conditions such as high blood pressure. My Swedish friend told me that in her country some doctors hand their patients this prescription: *walk for twenty minutes daily.*

Gratitude. How many of us feel tremendous gratitude to our National Health Service? How many of us leave the hospital or doctor's surgery feeling thankful for the doctor or consultant we just saw – even if we had to wait a little while? How many patients feel grateful for their expensive hospital tests and subsequent treatment? And for those who live in rural areas, do you appreciate the doctor you called out in the middle of the night and who travelled through adverse weather conditions to reach you?

In poorer countries some patients share beds. Yet in Britain if there's a bed shortage (usually because there is an emergency) and we have to wait a day or two, people complain bitterly. In this country we have some of the top clinicians in Europe working in our health service. We are exceedingly fortunate because we have unlimited access to their expertise.

And I mustn't forget the dentist. How many of us act responsibly by cancelling our appointment ahead of time instead of just not turning up? By acting irresponsibly we not only contribute to the waste in the health service, we also deny someone else who might have benefited from treatment sooner. This behaviour comes from a person who lacks gratitude.

Over the years, more and more scientists, doctors, and psychologists (especially in countries like America and India) are encouraging patients to develop an attitude of gratitude. They tell their patients that it is good for their spiritual, mental and physical well-being. These scientific minds have been combining ancient teachings and modern medical research to prove that one of the quickest and most direct routes to restoring health, harmony and balance in our lives is to cultivate the habit of gratitude and appreciation.

We are each gifted with 86,400 seconds a day. How many do you use to express gratitude?

The Terminally Ill

This work would not be complete without mentioning those who are terminally ill; those who, according to one doctor, can no longer be helped, medically. He said a certain patient may say, "How long have I got?" It takes tremendous courage to ask that question. And it must be difficult to hear and accept the words: *"There is nothing more we can do for you."*

I've met a number of patients who shared their experiences with me when I was volunteering. The patients who no longer had any questions for their clinicians; those who said they just wanted to "go quietly". It was as if they had gracefully 'surrendered' to their reality, to the inevitable.

One soft-spoken Caribbean man in particular stands out in my memory. He'd been in hospital for a week or so before I met him. Week after week, he said how much he looked forward to my visits. He had no visitors, which in itself must have been extremely lonely and emotionally painful. When I walked in to the bay his eyes would bulge with delight. Childlike, he would gesture for me to sit and then proceed to share some of his life stories. There was much laughter.

This gentleman was always hopeful, always grateful. He spoke highly of his consultant, of the nurses. He would mention how clean the ward had been kept. "Every time the cleaners finish, I thank them. Every day." One afternoon, in the nick of time, I walked in to the ward as he was about to go home. He reached out and hugged me and whispered, "They can't do anything more for me. I don't know how long I've got." Our bodies shook. I lightly patted his back. He had courageously accepted his fate. As he headed towards the door he turned and looked at me and said: "I'm just going to make use of the time I've got left." Thumbs up! He had surrendered gracefully. I felt privileged to have met such a person, and would have been disappointed if we hadn't had that last encounter. Consequently, I left the ward feeling inspired by his fortitude.

In an earlier chapter I mentioned the late Lord Gould and his attitude towards his cancer. In an interview by Andrew Marr on BBC One (18.09.11) he spoke candidly about his cancer, and the fact that it had returned. Calmly, he said, "I accept I am dying from cancer." Even in the midst of what he called "the death zone, the final place", he was positive; and gave the impression of a man still in control of his destiny. He still was, as he put it, "on purpose"; even though he discovered – having asked the question *"how long have I got"* – that he had just three months to live.

Philip Gould passed away two months after that BBC interview. The Times (13.04.12) published an extract from his final book – *When I Die: Lessons from the Death Zone.*[1]

"Just as being told I had three months to live had been a much bigger shock than any bad news before, this new timetable, being told I might die in three days, is another quantum leap...

"I have no doubt that this pre-death period is the most important and potentially the most fulfilling and the most inspirational time of my life. In this world, conventional time becomes meaningless. You map your course according to the coordinates of emotion and feelings, compassion and love. I am approaching the door marked Death. What lies beyond it may be the worst of things — or the best of things. I believe it will be the best of things."

I was so inspired by Philip Gould's attitude I bought a copy of his book.

---

[1]When I Die – Lessons from the Death Zone by Philip Gould and published by Little Brown Book Group

The Human Spirit

"Every time you smile at someone, it is an action of love,
a gift to that person, a beautiful thing."
- Mother Teresa

The old saying goes *Laughter is the best medicine.* And this is certainly the belief held by Dr Madan Kataria, an Indian physician who came up with the idea of laughter clubs in Mumbai in 1998. He, too, participates in these laughter sessions. This integrated therapy has since caught the attention of some American scientists who are looking into the effects of laughter in the healing process. According to their findings, it boosts the immune system. Laughter clubs are now popping up across the globe. It is an effective way for people to come together, for them to transcend their differences, embrace each other's lives, and equally important, to have some good old fashioned fun.

But there's another very effective strategy in the healing process: helping others, acts of kindness; the development of the human spirit. I find it contrary when I hear people say that by giving to themselves they're somehow being selfish; yet on the other hand they find it so difficult to extend kindness to others, especially strangers. Do we mainly give out of a sense of duty or pity? Perhaps we have a lot to learn from Third World communities where sharing is second nature. I was raised on one such community. It wasn't until I travelled to the 'developed' world that I realised how selfish people were. From my observation, there is a lack of social care, and courtesy, two very important components to building a healthy world.

In many parts of the world today people seem to be focusing on the acquisition of money, the accumulation of material possessions, greed. Generally speaking, there is a mis-guided belief that our happiness equals affordability, social status. How many people give because they want to make a positive contribution to society? Not enough.

Thousands of citizens do voluntary work. Some in hospitals, while a great many work with the bereaved, in hospices, and with the elderly. And there are many parents who encourage others who are in a similar situation, in spite of the fact that they may have lost their child, or that their child might be disabled, for instance. Some see it as their 'duty' to mentor young offenders; while others choose to work in youth clubs. A number of doctors and surgeons, in spite of their gruelling workload, do voluntary work in third world countries with aid organisations like Save the Children, Oxfam, and others.

Psychologists call these 'acts of kindness' stress busters. Why? Because not only does it put a smile on the face of the recipient, it lightens the heart of the giver. Nothing heals – emotionally or psychologically – like helping others. It is a powerful drug. The only prescription needed is an open heart, a kind word, a helping hand, trust, or just a smile.

Personally, I found doing voluntary work immensely rewarding. It gave me the opportunity to sit with patients, listen to their concerns; hold the hands of those whose operations were cancelled at the last minute leaving them feeling anxious. Instead of criticising the system, or blaming the surgeon, I would share jokes; anything to lighten their anxiety and help them see the positive side of the situation. Spending time with someone who is ill doesn't only help the patient, but it gives the volunteer an opportunity to be selfless, to show compassion. Volunteering, no matter where, or in what capacity, is a worthwhile commitment. Try it. It's a magical cure. It is one of the things to do before you die.

Tiffany spent the last week of her life in the Royal Brompton Hospital. Practically all her life she had been under the care of some of the top paediatric cardiologists in Europe. In spite of being in the best place for her problem, nothing more could be done for her. Was I bitter? No. Did I feel that the medical staff could have done more? The care couldn't have been better.

A couple of years later I decided to do voluntary work at the hospital as my way of giving back and saying 'thank you' for the best medical care one could have hoped for. Another contribution was donating her body to science. It was a decision her dad and I were happy to make. We believed that our small gesture will come together with others and one day cardio-scientists will be able to pinpoint the causes of the problem. Hopefully, with each discovery, they will be able to treat, quite successfully, young children suffering from rare heart and lung problems like hers and others.

After three years I moved on from doing voluntary work at the hospital. But I will always believe in the value of service. As a patient I still sit in hospital waiting rooms, and continue to observe patients' fears, their body language; their complaints as they wait their turn to be called. I continue to reach out and encourage, even if only one individual.

When I hear people complain about their health, their doctors, the hospitals or the National Health Service, or having to wait, my ears perk up! And by the time I've had a conversation with them, by the time I've helped them understand something (not about their medical condition) about their attitude, their impatience; the possibility that it could be their fear; or how fortunate they are to have first class treatment, I notice an immediate shift in their perspective. Mostly they smile. All complaints cease. It's as if their anxiety, their nervousness, just melts away in the moment. They've understood something that had previously eluded them.

Our contributions to the well-being of our society don't need to be grand; they won't necessarily be broadcast, or receive great applause. But every contribution, no matter how small, will be a positive step towards better health. Irrespective of our race, culture, religion, sexual orientation, gender or personality, we can all make a huge contribution to society. We're all capable of cultivating the habit of gratitude. They are fewer things in life that are as powerful as gratitude. Why not write a letter or call someone who has done something good for you and tell them how grateful you are. On the other hand, why not forgive someone you felt did you wrong. Resentment is crippling.

I remain confident that those of us who have gone beyond traditional beliefs, those who have empowered themselves, will be encouraged to reach out and support those who feel inadequate and fearful; those who believe that their illness is their doctor's business and not necessarily their own.

Those Who Inspired Me

It would be a dishonour not to add a few more potent ingredients to the soup: some of the women whose extraordinary courage has inspired me. Women like Anne, whom I met in 1998, the day I had my cardiac catheterisation (a special X-ray investigation which uses a dye to allow detailed pictures of the coronary arteries to be taken). I had once equated her slowness of movement with someone of a much more advanced age. Nor had I ever seen such large ankles wrapped in purple veins, as if all her veins had agreed to meet there. She'd had two heart valves replaced three times over the years. The first time was at age twenty-one.

Enviably knowledgeable, Anne explained that the tissue surrounding the valves was now threadbare. To illustrate, she described it as a piece of cloth that had been stitched and unpicked in the same place over and over until it was no longer of use. Her only hope was a heart transplant. She had been on the list for nearly two years.

"What will happen if a donor is not found?" I asked, curiously.

"Then I'll simply die," she said, without the slightest feeling of bitterness or betrayal by some external force. "I'm fifty and my daughter is twenty-four. It would have been dreadful had she been four."

Anne, the woman in the bed opposite mine, crippled by her failing heart, the woman whose survival depended on another person's death, lying reading and talking and laughing and sharing with the women on the ward was a great inspiration. It was difficult to feel sorry for such a positive and cheerful individual. Most encouraging was the fact that she wasn't afraid of death.

Just as I was about to be discharged the following morning, Anne asked if I'd studied the diagram of the heart that was posted on the wall. I hadn't.

So out of bed she got and slowly made her way to the diagram by the nurses' station for our tutorial. Her courage and resilience, her fearless approach to her illness, to life, made her my first 'hospital heroine'.

In October 2002 I was in Barbados when I had a mini stroke (transient ischemia attack – a TIA). Observing the other women on the ward, the temporary lack of oxygen to my brain seemed like nothing by comparison. They were the *real* heroines. Once my speech had returned somewhat, I started talking to some of the other female patients. One woman in her early forties, whose brain tumour had returned, was due to have surgery for the third time. The daily injections were excruciatingly painful, she told me. Yet, she didn't complain. Instead, she resorted to humour. This courageous mother of three said she had decided not to have surgery a third time. Instead, she would let Providence decide her fate. Looking around the ward I felt honoured to be in the company of remarkable women like her.

During Tiffany's final week in London's Royal Brompton Hospital, I was an onlooker – nothing more, painful though it was. After a couple of days her tiny veins made drawing blood almost impossible. I could sense her agony as the phlebotomist searched desperately for a healthy vein. As a mother, I wanted to shout: take mine instead. In the end, all I could do was try my best to comfort her. The greatest lesson in this for me was accepting there was absolutely nothing I could have done to change anything in her life. Nothing.

We want to know that we are doing all we can for our loved ones, but there are some things that are completely out of our control, no matter how close the relationship. And perhaps our function is just to comfort, to reassure them of our love. It is impossible to change anything for anyone else. Just as impossible as trying to drink for them or sleep for them. A fact. A harsh reality.

Tiffany wasn't a hospital heroine; she was the greatest teacher I ever had. Mothering her for over twenty years, my life developed and blossomed, exposing many unique qualities and talents. Endurance and compassion top the list. I've often said that the best in me was born out of having a disabled child. People say that caring for such a child with such complex needs must be challenging. It is. But with that responsibility, comes a host of life-enhancing gifts.

During a conversation with an elderly patient on the day of my discharge after my own surgery, she said, like a wise old sage, that she believed my daughter came to me for two reasons: because she knew I wouldn't "throw her in the bin", and secondly, "because I would use what I've learnt to help others." A similar sentiment was voiced by the middle-aged patient in the bed next to Tiffany the day before she died: "You should write a book about your daughter. I bet you have some rich experiences". I told her I would do that.

Finally, I'd like to share what I learned from one of my other 'hospital heroines', Amy, a twenty-three-year-old cystic fibrosis patient. I had gone to the hospital that day to take her out Christmas shopping. It had been some eighteen months since I'd pushed a wheelchair. I looked forward to our little outing, and so did she. Amy was smart and wise beyond her young years. We enjoyed each other's company. We shared. Barely able to breathe, she told me that her older sister had died a couple of years earlier from the same disease. She was reluctant to say any more than that. Amy was profoundly aware of the fact that her journey on the road ahead would be short.

Amy's name had not long before been put on the transplant list. She was excited. She also knew the facts. As with Anne, I wanted to know how a young person felt with such a debilitating disease, for which there is no cure. So I dared to ask the question that appeared in my thoughts seemingly from nowhere: "What is the most important thing to you?"

Inhaling deeply from the cylinder to which she was permanently attached, she said: "Oxygen. If people would only realise how fortunate they are to be able to breathe unaided they wouldn't take life for granted." I saw Amy once after that. Now every time I hear the word oxygen – the element that makes us all the same – I thank her for sharing something so simple, yet so profound.

My Masterclass

When we view life with a positive attitude and with gratitude, a greater understanding develops. We feel inspired to take responsibility. And during this process participation in our illness slowly becomes a habit. This is the time for us *to make our illness our business.* Better still, *make our health a priority.*

Having realised that there is nothing blissful about ignorance, a great number of patients will be less inclined to view their health from the observatory – from a distance; emotionally detached from reality. Instead they will be inspired by the old adage *knowledge is power.* And this new-found power will lead to confidence, which will in turn lead to healthier lives and empowered patients. According to Dr Christiane Northrup** *"You have the power to control your health."* She goes on to ask: *"Are you listening to your body's messages?"* www.drnorthrup.com**

In 2006 my daughter's body was donated to science. The day her dad and I signed the consent form I told the young doctor present, "I would like a copy of the post-mortem report. It will give me closure." Those words came seemingly from nowhere. Over the days and weeks, I waited apprehensively for the envelope to come through the door. Surprisingly, it was the one thing that had unnerved me most about Tiffany's death. Knowing how she died.

Once the report was in my hands I waited some days before peering at its contents. Not that I understood most of what was written; it was the report itself, the anatomical breakdown of my daughter's body that had caused my stomach to churn. Fear, as I have learned from personal experience as well as from coaching clients over the years, is usually greater than the reality. And these terrifying thoughts often appear real. I would pick up the report, retrieve the five pages, replace them, and put it down again. And again. Plucking up the courage one day, I began to study the post-mortem report along with the medical notes that I'd also requested cataloguing Tiffany's last week in hospital.

"How could you do that? It's a bit gruesome, don't you think?" one lady said, with a look of disgust.

"I wanted to know. Knowing stops me from convulsing with fear," I responded. "Knowing helps me to heal and gives me a greater awareness. Knowing is an education that takes me way beyond what I'd been taught. And quite frankly, what I'd been taught has taught me nothing."

The lady listened thoughtfully.

"And for me," I added, "without understanding there can be no closure."

The day after I'd had the courage to look at those pages, I got on the computer and spent hours looking up the medical terminology. I tried to put the pieces together. I got lost in my medical education, totally forgetting it was my daughter's body I was researching. I gained some insight into the complexity of the heart and the countless things that could go wrong with it. It was fascinating.

With this whiff of knowledge, I vowed to take better care of my own heart. The expression 'life is fragile' suddenly seemed real. Perhaps it was because I was in my mid-fifties. Now, six years on, I believe the earlier we start to see this truth the better. Leave it too long and it could be too late - too late to break old negative habits, too late to cultivate new beliefs and habits that empower us. That *can't teach an old dog new tricks* mindset should become obsolete. It has no positive attributes.

Once I'd understood, if only a little, the fear and heaviness that I'd been carrying lightened moment-by-moment. And it wasn't long before the words of the young woman doctor came flooding into my thoughts. "From now on this is not Tiffany. Everything will be referred to as tissue."

My emotions took a back seat the moment I understood what she meant. And, with my eyes transfixed on the computer screen, I heard myself whispering, "This is not Tiffany, this is matter."

Nothing beats knowing. This has been one of the most powerful experiences I've ever had.

I'd like to add another ingredient. It's something Professor Robert Winston, emeritus professor at Imperial College, said in a television documentary. *"What distinguishes us (human beings) from all other species is our inquisitiveness.* Remember, curiosity builds confidence, little-by-little.

A Lasting Legacy

I often listen to Dr Bruce Lipton, an American cell biologist. He, like so many other American scientists, is using images of the organs to help people understand why it is necessary for us to heal both ways: inside and out. In one of his lectures he told his audience that "cells do not act independently, but as a community."

It is clear that we are not alone. Whatever the situation, chances are many others are experiencing, or have experienced, the same thing. We all want better health, a better healthcare system. But none of us can do this alone. Everyone must chip in and take responsibility for their actions. It is important for us to leave things better than we found them for future generations.

The other day I was on my walk through a leafy south London area with its grand Victorian houses and lovingly tended front gardens when I was 'led' down one particular street. I said led because I know the area very well but had seldom walked down that street. It was late afternoon, just before the daylight faded, when I spotted a handwritten message pinned to the window with these words:

"Dear Mr Cameron, You're making a big mistake with the NHS. Please, please, please listen to us."

I returned to the house the following day to have a chat with the individual who felt so strongly about this matter. The elderly gentleman who answered the door said "She's at the demonstration." It was a demonstration of 15,000+ people expressing their anger about the closure of the accident and emergency department of a leading south London hospital. The idea to close this unit was insane. But then again, governments make decisions that arouse people's anger and cause them to demonstrate. Fundamentally, demonstrations are people's way of taking action, venting their anger in the hope that those responsible will listen and reverse their decisions.

Walking back to my flat, I thought of something I'd read by Maya Angelou in which she recounts the day the actress Shelley Winters showed up to lend a hand backstage in preparation for one of Dr Martin Luther King's rallies. Shocked, Dr Angelou asked her white friend, "Shelley, what are you doing here?" Without hesitation, Shelley said: "I have a daughter and one day she is going to look at me and ask: what did you do?"

As we know, Dr King led scores of blacks across America in the struggle against racial inequality. As is the nature of these uprisings and protests, although Dr King, like Ghandi, believed in non-violence, some demonstrators disagreed and resorted to violence.

One of those angry protestors was Eddie, a tall handsome young man whom I met in 1975 when he introduced me to Buddhism. It was hard to believe that this 'ray of sunshine' – as I've often described him – had spent four years in prison. He told me that he, along with an army of angry, impatient, young men and women were caught up in 'the revolution' as they marched from Brooklyn to Manhattan armed with machine guns. During this "say it loud; I'm black and I'm proud" era, Eddie believed that he had at least taken action. "Prison was the best thing to have ever happened to me," he told me one morning. Puzzled, I asked, "Prison"? "Yes. One day I had a deep awakening: it is peace and dialogue not violence that will change things for the better. So my 'struggle' now is for world peace." He then proceeded to share his new motto: "Trust through friendship; peace through trust."

Today, people the world over want justice and to oust unfair regimes. They are angry, they want to be heard and want satisfaction, at whatever cost. Closer to home, we want to 'Save Our NHS'. So some march, some send letters to politicians, while a great many take a more sedentary approach – they watch it on television or read about it in the newspapers. Of course we should challenge governments, voice our objections, even vote them out of office.

George Bernard Shaw said, *"People are always blaming their circumstances for what they are. I don't believe in circumstances. The people who get on in this world are the people who get up and look for the circumstances they want, and if they can't find them, make them."*

Leading modern-day thinkers would argue that blaming politicians (and doctors) for not 'creating the right circumstances', for not 'healing' us is not as organic, holistic or wholesome as each person taking responsibility and playing a small, yet vital, part.

Have you ever noticed how many mistakes politicians make? The number of times they change their minds, their policies, or blame the party opposite? Likewise, doctors haven't all the answers. So why then do so many people believe that they are the powerful ones? Why not place trust in ourselves because in the end we are the ones who must determine what kind of communities and what kind of health service we'd like. There is a saying *a drop of water will join others to form a great ocean*. With cell-like action, we must consciously work as a community. There is nothing wholesome about pessimism.

In Dr King's famous speech on the March on Washington in 1963 he told America, "I have a dream". Lasting change takes time, patience. Since that period in American history we've seen Dr King's dream come to pass. They're now African-American doctors, businessmen and women, congressmen and women, senators, mayors of large cities, including Atlanta, his hometown. Some are great community leaders embracing young people living in violent neighbourhoods. African-Americans now own their own homes; some work on Wall Street. The biggest dream of all is an African-American president, voted into office twice by blacks and whites alike. Did Mrs Robinson, Michelle Obama's mother, a woman born and raised in a segregated America ever think she'd be living in the White House?

And there is Oprah Winfrey. Born and raised in the heartland of slavery. Today, the girl from Mississippi has become the most powerful African American woman in the world. She is also known to be one of the world's greatest philanthropists. Oprah has brought people of all races together. She tells her audiences what she knows for sure: if you believe it, then you can do it. It's possible!

A friend sent me an e-mail of the cover of the magazine Black Business News, the Inauguration edition. There was a powerful image of Barak Obama, a black and white photo of Dr Martin Luther King, with the White House as its backdrop and the words CHANGE HAS COME.

When I took my white husband to New York back in 1981 I was very nervous. We stayed with my maternal grandmother in Bedford-Stuyvesant, one of Brooklyn's notoriously dangerous black neighbourhoods at the time. Having lived there for a number of years, I anticipated remarks such as honky, and worse. I warned him against doing the 'Englishman abroad' number! One couldn't be a tourist in ghettos like Brooklyn or Harlem; sightseeing was at one's peril.

The same was true of Britain in areas like Notting Hill and Brixton in London. A mixed-race couple walking those streets was unheard of. Today, it doesn't seem to matter. Bed-Stuy – as it's commonly called – like Notting Hill, has become a trendy, upmarket area where people from all walks of life have integrated. But this does mean that all racial issues have been resolved? Of course not. Some communities still live this way. Change is ongoing, so is prejudice and intolerance. There has to be something for the next generation to do, to learn from and pass on. They, too, must have the opportunity to add their own ingredients to the soup.

Sometimes life presents us with dire circumstances through which we have the opportunity to allow our curiosity to unfold. Normally, we prefer safe, easy. And when it turns out to be more challenging than we'd anticipated, we view the situation as dangerous, something or someone working against me. So we end up blaming others instead of seizing that opportunity for change.

I moved to America in 1970 at age twenty at the tail-end of the racial unrest. Within hours of arriving I was faced with a challenge I'd never anticipated: crime, squalid streets, angry people, people addicted to drugs and men and women swigging alcohol from bottles in brown paper bags. My fifty-something-year-old grandmother, glued to the television news, would warn me of the dangers of Brooklyn.

On her list of 'what not to do' were the streets, the muggings, the subways, and talking to people. "Mind your own business. You never know where the bullet will come from or who might stab you," she would warn. But in spite of her caution, I would go about my daily life somewhat like Alice in Wonderland looking for White Rabbit. Seduced by the energy and courage of the people, the sense of hope they portrayed, my confidence spiked to an unimaginable level. Moreover, being in that environment taught me that with 'people power' even the unthinkable is possible. The French have a saying *'l'impossible n'est rien'* – *the impossible is nothing.*

Dr King also said, *"Human progress is neither automatic nor inevitable... Every step toward the goal of justice requires sacrifice, suffering, and struggle; the tireless exertions and passionate concern of dedicated individuals."*

Instead of anger and dissatisfaction, let's embrace the spirit of Dr King's words and encourage each other to embrace our health service as an ongoing construction project. When building, every structure requires a team of professionals and helpers: funders, architects, site managers, project managers, masons, carpenters, plumbers, electricians, brick layers, labourers. In order to achieve their goal, all these people must transcend their differences and work in unity as a community. Let's follow this method and work towards achieving the best possible results.

Finally, let's remember that good health, whether physical, financial, mental or emotional, starts with, and is determined, consciously or unconsciously, by each individual and his or her actions, attitudes and beliefs. The notion that because we pay into the healthcare system it is somehow our right to take access to it for granted is misguided. Unless, of course, that's the structure, the inheritance, you wish to pass on to future generations. The choice is yours.

So, what type of structure will you commit to build? Remember the three little pigs? In the meantime, let George Bernard Shaw's words inspire you, or at least give you something to think about.

"This is the true joy in life, the being used for a purpose recognized by yourself as a mighty one. The being a force of nature, instead of a feverish, selfish little clod of ailments and grievances complaining that the world will not devote itself to making you happy.

"I am of the opinion that my life belongs to the whole community, and as long as I live, it is my privilege to do for it whatever I can. I want to be thoroughly used up when I die – for the harder I work, the more I live. I rejoice in life for its own sake. Life is no 'brief candle' to me; it is a sort of 'splendid torch', which I have got hold of for the moment, and I want to make it burn as brightly as possible before handing it on to future generations."

Resting – a Powerful Tonic

Learn to get in touch with the silence within yourself and know that everything in this life has a purpose.
- Elisabeth Kubler-Ross M.D. (1926 – 2004) Swiss American Psychiatrist

So far I haven't addressed a very import component to vibrant health – resting, meditation, living life in the slow lane and the healing properties therein. This idea may be foreign to some, but this age-old practise of stillness and meditation in some form or other is a way of connecting with a deeper part of ourselves. Yogis, Buddhist monks, clergymen /women and spiritual teachers practise the art of stillness and periods of silence. They know the beneficial properties in this daily ritual.

One thing that became crystal clear during my twenty-year stint as a mother of a disabled child is that it is impossible to give from an empty cup. Having to toss many balls in the air at the same time can be physically, mentally and emotionally draining. Feeling like they're trapped in a maze, some people wonder if 'this is their lot' in life.

Tired and exhausted, what can you genuinely give? Are you someone who feels that it's possible to be 'all things to all people'? Why do you find it so difficult to say NO? Do you 'exist' out of sense of duty, obligation, or guilt? Perhaps you worry about how others will view you. So, out of politeness people say, "I don't want to offend anybody". Don't you find living with that belief hellishly burdensome? How is living this way affecting your health?

During my daughter's final week of life, lying in the bed diagonally across from hers in the high dependency unit was a young man in his late twenties looking terribly sorry for himself. We started to talk. This banker told me about his 'scare', the heart attack that caused him to take stock of his life. He had worked punishing hours, eaten unhealthy foods at unhealthy hours; and hadn't felt the need to see a doctor.

"It was all go. But not anymore," he said.

We usually equate heart attacks with older overweight men, not men in their 20s/30s.

On another occasion I met a woman in her early forties who'd had a heart attack a couple of days before. Though mild, this experience was frightening. This mother of three children under ten also ran a business from home.

"I didn't even realise it was a heart attack."

"I once read somewhere the symptoms in women differ from those in men. But why, why do you feel the need to busy yourself 24/7?"

"Even as a child I was driven. My parents had high expectations. But being in here, having the time to think has forced me to look at the way I live. I have three children. They need me." This super-mum started to cry. "I'm sorry."

"No need to apologise for being human," I said teasingly.

I've often wondered why the English middle and upper middle-classes, especially, find it so difficult to show their emotions. This stiff-upper-lip behaviour means they would rather choke on their tears than let them flow. Being vulnerable is a tough one for them. One thing's for sure, those dark, repressed emotions have to go somewhere. But where, and in what form do they eventually appear?

"Here's something to think about," I said, as I was about to leave her bedside. "Promise your children's mother that she will slow down and take greater care of herself! And, by the way," I added, "stop tucking in your emotions. It's bad for your heart!"

These patients are certainly not alone in the age of bigger, faster, more, more, more. There's the internet, mobile phones, money, shopping. Some people on a drive to copy celebrities are stressed and exhausted. I read an article that said more and more teenagers are so stressed and so ambitious they are suffering from depression and burning out prematurely.

Today, women of an advanced age see wrinkles as the enemy and are declaring war on aging. Growing old gracefully seems unfashionable in this fast-paced world of celebrity and firm flesh. As for grey hair, well! Whenever I see a woman with grey hair I make a point of telling her how beautiful she looks. The compliment lifts her spirits. I also like to know that I'm in good company! The fact is widely publicised that midlife women drink and smoke more than men because they're suffering from a low self-image, lacking in confidence and drowning in misery.

On the other hand, there is great admiration for the baby-boomers who are living out their dreams; they believe that life begins at sixty! I agree! Valuing life and good health, they do everything in their power to stay healthy. They (men included) believe that slow doesn't mean less, it improves quality. Some say they have the best sex lives ever! They are beacons of light with that 'less is more' mentality. They rarely see a doctor. Their positive energy and youthful spirit is not only infectious, it is a cut above the rest. Our society needs more like them.

My question is: does this hamster wheel lifestyle make people more successful, happier, or healthier? Wellbeing certainly isn't obvious to me when I go the hospital for my blood tests and check-ups. I invariably arrive to a sea of people. The ground floor of this large teaching hospital is reminiscent of a train station at rush hour. Usually, I have to negotiate my way round hoards of people trying to find their way to this or that department.

We've established that resting is a foreign concept in our culture. People are embarrassed to say they're taking a nap, or doing nothing during the day, if they are. Conditioned to believe they should be constantly on the go, they see napping, resting, as a pastime for the elderly, ill or infirmed, or someone in chronic pain. We are living in a world of chaos and hurry, and we burn out. One newspaper article I read recently said that half of the people in the UK are too stressed to sleep and the effects are taking a toll on their wellbeing.

Very few of us are aware of (or question) the psychological or physiological reasons for our symptoms like headaches, blood pressure, depression, sleepless nights, anxiety or worry. Some become fraught and end up blaming others or hit the bottle for comfort; others rush to the doctor, who in turn writes a prescription. Suppose resting is the answer? What if slowing down is the most effective way of repairing our bodies? Why do you think doctors tell patients to 'get plenty of rest'? Especially after an operation, a bout of serious illness and in some cases the flu. Prescriptions for rest should be more readily available!

Human beings have the tendency to become fearful and distraught when something major in their lives falls apart. But what if that's a good thing? What if it's a subconscious message that says, you're moving too fast, you're thinking too much, it's time to reassess the situation and take better care of your health? Would this be a freeing thought or would it make you feel like a failure, or even guilty?

Here are a few suggestions that could help you put life into perspective. Go for a walk. Sit in nature. Look at the wonder of creation, of life, just for the sake of it. We learned from childhood that sitting quietly and resting our thoughts and bodies is 'doing nothing', 'day dreaming', 'being lazy' or 'wasting time', even. As a result, we try to avoid doing so at all costs by 'doing something'. But what if doing nothing, being still, is one of the best remedies on the market? Don't wait until there is a health crisis. Listen to your body's messages. Listen to the sound of silence. Take a guilt-free afternoon nap. It's called self-preservation. What others think is their business.

Alternatively, why not jot down your feelings and thoughts in a journal daily. It is very therapeutic. Create a 'breathing space' just for you. Listen to classical or meditative music. Mindfully watch the raindrops on the window pane. Consciously feel your chest rise and fall as you breathe in and out. Close your eyes and drift.

Also, when outdoors, why not stop and listen to the wind, playfully feel the breeze on your skin, listen to the birds, watch them in flight. Rest your thoughts on the passing clouds. Or sit and watch young children at play in the park. When your thoughts overwhelm you, and they will, take some deep, refreshing breaths. Leave complaining behind and appreciate the fact that you're alive.

Resting our minds rejuvenates our bodies. So every day do something for you. It doesn't matter what practise you use as long as you are quiet, you are 'filling your cup'. Feel that your cup 'runneth over', and in this way you'll have enough energy to go around. Begin with as little as fifteen minutes and increase it slowly. I value the time I spend resting. It is far more than a daily ritual. It is a tonic I couldn't live without.

I did some work in a high security prison a few years back. A nineteen-year-old inmate, serving a life sentence, told me on one occasion: "When I look out at the fields and lush countryside, although I am 'behind bars', I am not. Sometimes, I sit idle and experience some pretty mind-blowing stuff. I feel happy, not locked in."

Psychologists and professionals in the field of mind-body medicine believe resting and meditation to be the ultimate remedy for the treatment of stress, depression, headaches, high blood pressure, insomnia and low self-esteem. So lock the door, kick off your shoes, put on some soothing music and chill. Don't forget to switch off your mobile phone!

It is important to mention that I am in no way suggesting resting, meditation and stillness as a replacement for prescription medication or medical advice. Throughout these pages I've stressed the importance of discussing one's medical issues with the relevant healthcare professional.

In an earlier chapter I mentioned that I'm on Warfarin, a medication that I and countless others can't live without. Cardiac surgery and Warfarin changed my life. I am exceedingly grateful. However, as powerful as the drug is, it cannot heal my emotions; it doesn't help me make decisions I need to make, or take the actions that need to be taken. This understanding continues to be the driving force behind all that I do.

On the other hand, because of it, I've become more discerning about my mortality. Being on Warfarin and living with the knowledge that my blood could be too thin or too thick, or that this could cause me to either bleed to death or have a massive stroke, is a juggling act. Not dis-similar to everyday life, it's a process.

I've spent many long hours walking and sitting in nature since being on Warfarin. Stillness keeps me centred and at peace. Being in nature has helped me understand the workings of life, and the fact that life is limitless. Consequently, I am no longer afraid or anxious. I've come to embrace the drug as my best friend. I've also learned to let go and not to be too concerned about what tomorrow holds. This is not to suggest that I don't have goals and dreams. I do. This awareness, this transformation, keeps me centred. I hold the view that things will work out as they're meant to. I also experience more joy. The more joy there is in my life the more I can share with others. Along with a healthy diet this is my prescription for a balanced life. The only 'must have' I crave is living well. Less has become more.

Sit quietly and ask yourself: what would I do if I had just six months to live? Make a list in order of priority. What's your next step?

Conclusion

I must tell you that I wasn't commissioned to write this book, nor have I had any financial assistance to help with its production. I could easily have said – why bother? Ultimately, it was my passion that kept me going. I was determined to play my part by using my twenty-plus years' experience looking after my daughter, plus my own health problems and years of research, to encourage others. It would have been a waste otherwise. So, why *not* bother!

Bringing this work to its conclusion hasn't been easy. There was always an irresistible urge to add another ingredient! Stories in the media, the press, research, a conversation with someone on the street, or whilst travelling on the bus; questions from an audience after giving a talk, personal insights, even my dreams, would further ignite my passion. One morning, at the crack of dawn, I jumped out of bed having dreamt of the moving experience the phlebotomist had shared.

There were the ongoing demonstrations about the health service; people wanting to SAVE OUR NHS. A great many of us want to save something; speak up and voice our opinions about that cause. And because people the world over react in more or less the same way, I decided to call this chapter *A Lasting Legacy* and write it from a broader perspective; a time in history. Why? I wanted to encourage people to think out of the box; I wanted them to believe that whatever they want to achieve in life with the right attitude and mindset – is possible. Doubt keeps people grounded in misery.

I also felt compelled to include the experience with my father-in-law. It is important for readers to understand that doctors are human, after all. So the chapter *Why It's Good to Talk* was born. And what about a chapter on 'service', a voice whispered. It is also important to remind people of the power in reaching out, in giving back. Helen Keller, (1880 – 1968) an American author who was both blind and deaf once said: *"The world is full of suffering. It is also full of the overcoming of it."* Her profound insights have long been a source of inspiration for me. So I had to share her pearls of wisdom with you. I believe she meant people like you and me reaching out and helping others. I know, you're saying all this reaching out and embracing others is not very British. See it is as an act of kindness to humanity and – just do it! All it takes is a commitment from you – one small step.

It's possible for us to overcome our fears; dare to trust, dare to believe. Change our outlook from what has always been to what we'd like to see now and in the future and our role in it. It's also possible to move forward instead of being stuck in that all too familiar 'comfort zone'. I've never quite understood why it is called such because people in this 'zone' give the impression of being miserable and imprisoned; trapped by fear and insecurity.

One day I received online access to the film *Hungry for Change – Your Health is in Your Hands.* I had to write a chapter highlighting some of the things I learned. I also wanted to end with an appropriate quotation, but couldn't think of one. One morning during my meditation, George Bernard Shaw's words sprang to mind.

Years ago, I used it to encourage clients and those who came to me for guidance complaining. I'd ask them what 'legacy' they would like to pass on; or what would they have to do in order to make their torch burn brightly? They hadn't thought of it. They were too busy complaining that the world would not make them happy, like those who complain about their hospitals, their doctors, the government, life. I also felt it essential to elaborate a bit more on fear. But I had to stop adding ingredients; turn off the fire; take the pot off the cooker – done!

I hope you've enjoyed the soup just as much as I've enjoyed making it! It has been a huge opportunity to learn new things and keep my curiosity alert. I'm confident that the more we practise and develop the power of inquisitiveness, the quicker we will harness the power of understanding and greater awareness. And this understanding will not only help us conquer our fears, but will undoubtedly lead to confidence, participation, and ultimately, healthy, empowered patients. Remember: it's possible!

One final ingredient! It is said that 'love cures all'. But first and foremost that loves has to begin with one's love for oneself. In other words, 'true love' begins within. Loving yourself is not about being vain; it is an essential component for healthy living. Think of it as lovingly a tending your garden – your inner garden. Picture for a moment a garden that is neglected; then picture garden that is lovingly tended. Which would you rather be?

Love for oneself is something we are rarely encouraged to do, or believe, in our society. Undoubtedly, love for oneself brings with it a huge dollop of self-respect, deep feelings of inner freedom, heaps of hope, a mega dosage of confidence and a poultice of self-belief, self-worth. Added to this effective prescription, this inside-out approach to healing is joy and laughter. So laugh, laugh, and laugh some more; spread joy for the heck of it! It's good for your health!

Recommendations

Books:

Doctor, Doctor: Incredible True Tales from a GP's Surgery
— Dr Rosemary Leonard

Healing from the Heart: — Dr Mehmet Oz

Seize the Day — Marie de Hennezel

The European Patient of the Future (State of Health) — Angela Coulter

The Everyday Diabetic Cookbook — Stella Bowling

Perfect Health: The Complete Mind/Body Guide — Dr Deepak Chopra

Happiness Now! Timeless Wisdom for Feeling Good Fast — Robert Holden

You Can Heal Your Life – Louise L Hay

Why People Don't Heal, and How They Can — Caroline Myss

Diabetes for Dummies (UK Edition)
— Alan L. Rubin MD & Dr. Sarah Jarvis GP

Warfarin & You — V. B. Blake

Motivational Interviewing in Health Care: Helping Patients Change Behavior
— Stephen Rolinick, William R. Miller & Christopher C. Butler

Beyond Sugar Shock: The 6-week Plan to Break Free of Your Sugar Addiction
— Connie Bennett

The Encyclopaedia Of Healing Foods
— Dr. Michael Murray, Dr. Joseph E. Pizzorno & Lara U. Pizzorno

Food is Better Medicine than Drugs
— Patrick Holford & Jerome Burne

Healing Hypertension: A Revolutionary New Approach – Samuel J Mann

All books are available through Amazon.

Talks:

Women's Bodies, Women's Health – Dr Christiane Northrup

Change Your Thoughts, Change Your Life - Dr Wayne Dyer

www.ted.com/talks/atul_gawande_how_do_we_heal_medicine?
www.ted.com/talks/brian_goldman_doctors_make_mistakes_can_we_talk_about_t
hat?

Note: One could be overwhelmed, even utterly confused, by the amount of information that is available. Being informed is hugely beneficial. It's about common sense and moderation. When in doubt run your findings pass your healthcare practitioner. And if you find something that works, why not share it with him/her.